What Does Justice Look Like

and Why Does

God Care about It?

THE JESUS WAY
—SMALL BOOKS *of* RADICAL FAITH—

What Does Justice Look Like

and Why Does
God Care about It?

JUDITH & COLIN MCCARTNEY

HERALD
PRESS

Harrisonburg, Virginia

Herald Press
PO Box 866, Harrisonburg, Virginia 22803
www.HeraldPress.com

Study guides are available for many Herald Press titles at www.HeraldPress.com.

WHAT DOES JUSTICE LOOK LIKE AND WHY DOES GOD CARE ABOUT IT?
© 2020 by Herald Press, Harrisonburg, Virginia 22803. 800-245-7894.
All rights reserved.
Library of Congress Control Number: 202094500
International Standard Book Number: 978-1-5138-0571-9 (paperback);
    978-1-5138-0620-4 (ebook)
Printed in United States of America
Cover and interior design by Reuben Graham

24 23 22 21 20   10 9 8 7 6 5 4 3 2 1

Contents

Introduction to The Jesus Way Series from Herald Press

The Jesus Way is good news for all people, of all times, in all places. Jesus Christ "is before all things, and in him all things hold together"; in him "all the fullness of God was pleased to dwell" (Colossians 1:17, 19). The Jesus Way happens when God's will is done on earth as it is in heaven.

But what does it mean to walk the Jesus Way? How can we who claim the name of Christ reflect the image of God in the twenty-first century? What does it mean to live out and proclaim the good news of reconciliation in Christ?

The Jesus Way: Small Books of Radical Faith offers concise, practical theology that helps readers encounter big questions about God's work in the world. Grounded in a Christ-centered reading of Scripture and a commitment to reconciliation, the series aims to enliven the service and embolden the witness of people who follow Jesus. The volumes in the series are written by a diverse community of internationally renowned pastors, scholars, and practitioners committed to the way of Jesus.

The Jesus Way series is rooted in Anabaptism, a Christian tradition that prioritizes following Jesus, loving enemies, and creating faithful communities. During the Protestant Reformation of the 1500s, early Anabaptists who began meeting for worship emphasized discipleship in addition to belief, baptized adults instead of infants, and pledged their allegiance to God over loyalty to the state. Early Anabaptists were martyred for their radical faith, and they went to their deaths without violently resisting their accusers.

Today more than two million Anabaptist Christians worship in more than one hundred countries around the globe. They include Mennonites, Amish, Brethren in Christ, and Hutterites. Many other Christians committed to Anabaptist beliefs and practices remain in church communities in other traditions.

Following Jesus means turning from sin, renouncing violence, seeking justice, believing in the reconciling power of God, and living in the power of the Holy Spirit. The Jesus Way liberates us from conformity to the world and heals broken places. It shines light on evil and restores all things.

Join Christ-followers around the world as we seek the Jesus Way.

Introduction

Recently, we had the opportunity to take some of the leaders of the ministry we serve to Atlanta to visit sites and museums that memorialize the life, struggle, and triumphs of Dr. Martin Luther King Jr. As we walked through Dr. King's church, visited his grave site, and took in the museum exhibits, we were challenged by real-life examples of the battle between **justice** and injustice. Most of us know about Dr. King's important accomplishments for social justice. But what these wonderful exhibits cannot fully reveal is the heartbeat inside the man that empowered him to fight for justice against all the odds.

What was it that fueled Dr. King's love for justice?

The answer is found in his faith. In Jesus, Dr. King saw a nonviolent champion for justice who spoke up for the poor and oppressed. As a Baptist minister, Dr. King also understood the foundational theme of justice found throughout all of Scripture. These things, along with his deep spiritual practices, empowered King to work for justice even when his enemies threatened his life.

Justice is important to God. Throughout Scripture we read of a God who cares about the poor and oppressed. Likewise, justice was central to the mission of Jesus, as is evident in this passage from Isaiah that Jesus read at the inauguration of his ministry: "The Spirit of the Lord is on me, because he has anointed me to proclaim good news to the poor. He has sent me to proclaim freedom for the prisoners and recovery of sight for the blind, to set the oppressed free, to proclaim the year of the Lord's favor" (Luke 4:18-19).

Note the proclamations at the heart of Jesus' mission: Good news for the poor. Freedom for the prisoners. Sight for the blind. Equality for the oppressed. These are signs of the year of the Lord's favor! Shouldn't we, as followers of Jesus, seek the same?

The purpose of this book is to encourage readers to develop a biblical understanding of justice. We've included theological foundations for justice along with real-life stories, practical examples, and reflection questions to help you live what you read. Judith and I (Colin) wrote this book together based on more than thirty-five years of experience in urban ministry. Colin provides teaching and theological ideas at the beginning of each chapter. Judith then writes from personal experience in the "Living It Out" section at the end of the chapter to help put flesh on the teaching through personal, real-life stories.

We've written this book for all who seek to follow Jesus in the way of justice. If your life experience and social location is primarily one of privilege, we hope this book will challenge you to take steps toward living in solidarity and seeking justice with those who have less power and privilege. The question the privileged must ask of themselves is, "What kind of human do I choose to be?" To benefit from injustice and allow it to continue, when you have power to make things right no matter the personal cost, is a moral issue that, left unresolved, will tear away at your soul. If you have suffered systemic injustice, we hope you hear clearly in this book Jesus' revolutionary proclamation of freedom for the oppressed and gain strength for the struggle for justice. It is our desire that what you read encourages you to know that God is on your side. And if, like many of us, your life experience includes both having privilege and suffering injustice, we hope this book will help you find a way to embrace Jesus' call both to liberation from oppression and to costly discipleship so that all may flourish.

We start this book in chapter 1 by contrasting the injustices in our world with God's original intention for our world to be a place that is very good for all people, not just for some. In chapter 2 we examine what went wrong in our world and how we become complicit in creating an environment of injustice that destroys people's lives. In chapter 3, we take a look at what justice looks like to God and its connection to God's desire for **shalom** in our world, defined as holistic peace and fairness for all people. (Key terms appear in bold and are defined in the glossary.) Chapter 4 tackles God's plan for restoring the fallen cosmos by looking at how Jesus enacted justice throughout his life and ministry. In chapter 5, we journey together through eight important traits of justice that we must embody and seek in our world today. The problem of **systemic injustice** is examined in chapter 6, as we discover ways we can combat this powerful and insidious evil that is deeply intertwined with our way of life. We finish the book with chapter 7, as we go further in understanding the responsibilities that religious, political, and economic leaders have in ensuring that justice is served and maintained within our societal structure.

Be encouraged and forewarned. In all our years of urban ministry, we have discovered that living out Jesus' call to justice is hard work. The greatest fire in our soul can begin to turn to ashes as a result of this exhausting work. And let's face it, being selfish, complacent, or just giving up about injustice is a lot easier for those of us who benefit from it than seeking what is right and fair for all people, not just some. Preparation and awareness are essential if we intend to live out God's commitment to justice. Those who are committed to following Jesus in his mission of justice in a hurting world need resources to sustain them so that they don't wear themselves out or slip back into a self-centered life. And those who seek liberation from the oppression of injustice in their own lives and communities need empowerment, affirmation, and hope to continue in the struggle. This is why we hope this book will help you to build a sustainable, holistic, and sacred pathway to pursuing justice with God and the community around you.

Now, with a focus on Jesus as our source and passion, we pray that what you read will guide you as you seek God's reign of justice in our world today.

1

The Way It Is Supposed to Be

The temperature was climbing as I (Colin) stepped gently along narrow pathways among hovels whose inhabitants stared up at me with fearful and empty eyes. All around me were hungry people with bloated stomachs, helpless mothers holding crying babies, angry men, and many young people living together in a sea of filth. These are the forgotten ones, precious to God but ignored by humanity, forced to build their homes on a garbage dump in the middle of the bustling city of Santo Domingo in the Dominican Republic.

As I slowly made my way past makeshift homes, I repeatedly stepped over oozing garbage that poured from the refuse dump like dripping sweat. Throughout my journey in this slum, I continually prayed silently, "Our Father, who is in heaven, hallowed be your name. Your kingdom come, your will be done, on earth, right here, in this garbage dump, as it is in heaven."[1]

There is something terribly wrong in our world when people are living in garbage dumps, scavenging for food. The immense worth of these precious people has been rejected by consumeristic global economic systems that value some lives more than others. In such a world, some people are considered disposable, or economic burdens. When this happens, injustice reigns in their lives. In the modern world, children should not die from hunger-related sickness, but they do! More than 3.1 million children die each year from hunger and its effects.[2]

We all claim to want equality, yet we continue to see racism and sexism rear their ugly heads while many of us ignore the reality that a disproportionate number of people of color experience incarceration and poverty. We claim to be open-minded, but many people continue to discriminate against others because of gender, sexual orientation, or religious beliefs. These acts of injustice occur every day.

Our world was never supposed to be this way.

God has always intended for our world to be just and fair, an Edenic paradise. Right from the start, God created beauty from empty darkness. Genesis says: "In the beginning God created the heavens and the earth. Now the earth was formless and empty, darkness was over the surface of the deep, and the Spirit of God was hovering over the waters" (Genesis 1:1-2).

In the story of creation in Genesis, God transforms dark chaos into a peaceful paradise and then declares that the world, the way it is supposed to be, is very good. The Scripture says, "God saw what he had made, and it was very good" (Genesis 1:31).

God brings life-giving symmetry into darkness, creating humanity and nature to exist together in perfect harmony.

All of creation is in right relationship and at peace with God and one another. In the garden of Eden, life is just, with no hunger, no killing, no oppression, no suffering. All of creation is valued, sacred, esteemed, and treated equally, with utmost respect. All is well and whole, and lacking nothing. This is what God describes as being "very good," and this is what God's justice looks like. Whenever the world misses this mark of God's definition of being "very good," it is unjust.

When we see our world through the lens of God's declaration that all of creation is "very good," we are able to see a deeper reality in our world than we otherwise would. By having a Genesis 1 perspective, we are able to discern what is just because we know God's original intent and ultimate purpose for people and our environment. A just world reflects God's original intention for all of creation to be in right relationship and at peace with God and one another. Justice honors everything God creates as sacred, including all of humanity, which is endowed with great value as ones who are created "in the image of God" (Genesis 1:27).

Whenever we harm our environment or degrade the value of people, we deface God's original intention for creation, and this is a great injustice. With this in mind, Martin Luther King Jr. describes justice in his famous "Letter from a Birmingham Jail" by referring to God's moral and eternal law established in God's original declaration that creation is "very good." King writes:

> How does one determine whether a law is just or unjust? A just law is a man-made code that squares with the moral law or the law of God. An unjust law is a code that is out of harmony with the moral law. To put it in the terms of St. Thomas Aquinas: An unjust law is a human law that is not rooted in eternal law and natural law. Any law that

uplifts human personality is just. Any law that degrades human personality is unjust.[3]

Sadly, injustice continues to be perpetrated every day. Our environment is pillaged, and people are oppressed. When sin entered the world, it brought grave injustice.[4]

God's "very good" creation is now constantly under attack. God's Edenic purpose has now been infected with the poisonous effects of sin. What God declared to be "very good" is now permeated with shame, division, violence, selfishness, oppression, and environmental damage. All that God declared to be "very good" is vulnerable to injustice, which threatens to make it into something that is "very bad."

It was never supposed to be this way.

A view of the world shaped by Genesis 1 will embolden us with a heart for justice and a desire for the restoration of all creation to its state of being "very good." With Genesis 1 eyes, we are able to respond to the marring of a "very good" creation and join God's ongoing work to return our cosmos to its original state of goodness for all people. By doing this, we fulfill God's original calling for humans to be stewards of creation. This means it is our God-given responsibility to be just and to work for justice for all of God's creation, including humankind.[5]

When Jesus taught his disciples to pray, he did so with Genesis 1 eyes. Jesus challenged them to join him in asking God that "your kingdom come, your will be done, on earth as it is in heaven" (Matthew 6:10).

God is yearning for his kingdom to fully come and for his will to be done, right here on earth. God yearns for a world in which everyone is treated equally and fairly, where there is no more hunger, chaos, or oppression. Heaven on earth, a world that is "very good," has always been the will of God.

The prophet Isaiah saw the world with Genesis 1 eyes. He saw that God intends to restore all of creation to its original goodness when he wrote these words from God, addressed to Israel:

> See, I will create new heavens and a new earth. The former things will not be remembered, nor will they come to mind. . . . I will rejoice over Jerusalem and take delight in my people; the sound of weeping and of crying will be heard in it no more. Never again will there be in it an infant who lives but a few days, or an old man who does not live out his years; the one who dies at a hundred will be thought a mere child; the one who fails to reach a hundred will be considered accursed. They will build houses and dwell in them; they will plant vineyards and eat their fruit. No longer will they build houses and others live in them, or plant and others eat. For as the days of a tree, so will be the days of my people; my chosen ones will long enjoy the work of their hands. They will not labor in vain, nor will they bear children doomed to misfortune; for they will be a people blessed by the LORD, they and their descendants with them. Before they call I will answer; while they are still speaking I will hear. The wolf and the lamb will feed together, and the lion will eat straw like the ox, and dust will be the serpent's food. They will neither harm nor destroy on all my holy mountain, says the LORD (Isaiah 65:17, 19-25)

As followers of Jesus, the challenge for us today is this: What can we do to bring about Isaiah's vision and the longing of the Lord's Prayer for heaven on earth? How are we to be citizens of the **kingdom of God** in an age in which the kingdom of heaven is present but not yet fully realized?[6]

There is much to be done, so let's jump right in and see how we can join Jesus in bringing about God's kingdom "on earth as it is in heaven."

LIVING IT OUT

We live in a world where things can go terribly wrong. Yet our Father wants restoration and wholeness right here on earth. We are people of hope, enabled to see our world with Genesis 1 eyes that allow us to cut through the present chaos and see the reality of a God who created everything "very good." We must reflect God's Genesis 1 lens in today's world. Injustice continues, and there will always be lots to do to bring about justice. But to do so, we need to slow down and do some soul work so that our actions are aligned with what our heavenly Father is doing in our world.

I (Judith) grew up as an immigrant in a new country. My family is originally from Indonesia and moved to a rural town in Canada. We looked different from anyone else in our small town and our struggle to learn English didn't help much with fitting in. We faced discrimination just because we were different. At the time we didn't have much, but we had sound values, including kindness and a desire to help others. We worked hard in all we did and yet we didn't have a conventional faith in God. We didn't go to church, we didn't have churchgoing friends, and we didn't give money to a church, but my mother had a simple faith in God. She never spoke of it, but I saw a few storybooks about God that awakened my curiosity, and my soul started to stir. At a time when I was searching spiritually, someone from a church bus ministry knocked on our door to see if anyone in our family would like to attend Sunday school. That was my official introduction to church. My curiosity grew a little bit more. While this was happening, my father was beginning to make good money as a trucker. Life slowly was getting better for us, but then tragedy struck. When I was eleven years old, my mother experienced a brain aneurysm. She was in a coma for a little while before she died.

The loss was great. I had seven siblings, including a toddler of two as well as young adults in their mid-twenties.

My father wasn't with us when my mother was rushed to the hospital; he was far away on the road making a delivery. He received a call on his CB radio telling him to get off at the nearest truck stop and call home because there was an emergency. All alone at a truck stop, my father found out that his wife was in a coma, dying from a brain aneurysm. With tears streaming down his face, my father began to plead with the people around him to help him get to the nearest airport. He knew he had to be with his wife before she passed away. However, the people either ignored him or rudely told him to speak proper English. No one there helped my father, and he collapsed into a nearby booth and wept. A woman saw my dad in his state of grief and, though she didn't know my father, sat down beside him and asked if he needed help. My father wept as he shared the tragic news with this complete stranger. She comforted him and prayed for him and my family. Then she went out of her way to drive my father to the airport and help him book a flight so he could be with his dying wife and grieving children. This woman was like an angel sent by God to help him at this tragic time, and he never forgot her kindness. She was the hands and feet of Jesus to my hurting father.

We had lost the heartbeat and the life of our home, my mother. Soon after my mom died, my father had major health issues and our middle-class family quickly became poor once again. On top of the scarcity and racism we experienced as newcomers to Canada, we now struggled in our grief. At times we felt that we didn't measure up to other families, and we were well aware of the stares and sneering some people expressed toward us. Though we were made to feel like outsiders and dismissed by some people, the local church, full of people we did not know, gathered around our family and supported us through these dark days and in the years to come. Church members visited us, befriended my family, and helped provide for our needs. Some of the seniors adopted us as their grandchildren, groceries were dropped off at our porch, and some people even paid for my sister and I to attend a private school. These wonderful people never made us feel inferior because we weren't white, spoke broken English, or held to different customs. They saw us as important to God and thus important to them and responded with practical acts of kindness. They also knew that it would be a great injustice if they, who had plenty, were to ignore our family, who had little. So they acted justly by caring for us. These Christians lived out the words of the prophet Micah, who said, "He has shown you, O mortal, what is good. And what does the LORD require of you? To act justly and to love mercy and to walk humbly with your God" (Micah 6:8).

Though this is a sad story, something very good happened in the midst of it. My family began to attend church. My father never forgot the kindness he experienced through the Christians who came into his life. The woman at the truck stop and the people of the local church who surrounded our family in our time of need had left their mark on all of us. The curiosity of my soul also deepened even more, and surrounded by Christians who acted justly on behalf of our family, I started to fall in love with my new friend, Jesus, who cared for the hurting and the poor. I remember this experience as rich and wonderful. It is a memory that I return to when I need to reorient myself in the busyness of my life.

The loss of my mother and the many experiences I encountered during those dark days launched me into a life of caring for others who suffer. My relationship with Jesus that was birthed through the influence of loving Christians now drives my passion to work to bring about social justice for the poor and vulnerable in urban settings. Because of my own suffering and the experience I had with Christians who really cared for us in our time of need, I have a special empathy for those who are far too often ignored. Through all of this, I encountered Jesus as more than a personal savior of souls, but also a lover of the poor and neglected. That realization resulted in intense spiritual transformation in my life. From my experience I now know that the closer I am to Jesus, the more I am empowered to help bring transformation into the lives and communities of those who suffer. I slowly realized that it was Jesus who drove the behavior of those Christians who did not know my family but were inspired to help us. I understand that inner work precedes outer actions. Only a Jesus-filled life can help bring about Jesus-like justice to those who suffer.

If we want to bring wholeness and healing to others, before we seek the restoration of a community through justice, we must first allow Jesus to bring his healing to our own souls. In this way, justice starts with us. As we extend the peace of Christ, let us first make sure that his peace reigns in our hearts. Like me, we all could use a memory of an encounter with Jesus and his justice that will help to reorient us to a sacred time of soulful simplicity.

2

What Went Wrong?

We have emphasized the need to view the world through the lens of Genesis 1 so we can see the way that things are meant to be "very good." Unfortunately, many Christians tend to view the world through a negative lens based on the fall of humanity as seen in Genesis 3. The problem with this approach is that, when our perception of the world begins with Genesis 3 instead of Genesis 1, we see life through the lens of the curse of sin and injustice. Looking at the world through the wrong lens distorts our view of our world. When we view the world through the lens of the curse of Genesis 3, our perspective inevitably leads to cursing ourselves, others, and our environment. This reality is reflected in the Genesis story in which our ancestors turned their "very good" life into a "cursed life," allowing sin to have far-reaching environmental and social impacts.

In Genesis 3 we read that Adam and Eve were tempted by the serpent to disregard the source of all blessings in order to "be like God, knowing good and evil" (Genesis 3:5). Eve, with Adam right by her side, "saw that the fruit of the tree was good for food and pleasing to the eye, and also desirable for gaining wisdom, she took some and ate it. She also gave some to her husband, who was with her, and he ate it. Then the eyes of both of them were opened" (Genesis 3:6-7).

The story of the fall of humanity is a tragic case study that demonstrates how injustice begins. Each temptation that Adam and Eve faced represents a powerful trigger that can set unjust actions in motion. Humans were created to trust God, not to be gods. In our humanity, we struggle with the same four temptations that Adam and Eve embraced. If we try to take them on with our own strength, we only end up expanding them into acts of great injustice. Be warned! We face the same temptations as our ancestors of old, but through the story of the fall, we have ample caution regarding their implications.

FOUR TEMPTATIONS THAT LEAD TO INJUSTICE

1. To Be Like God

To be our own god means we are answerable to no one. As a god, our desires, wishes, and wants are our right, even if they take place at the expense of others or the environment. Humans cannot handle this kind of responsibility without harming others, and history is filled with people who have been corrupted by such power. As the British historian Lord Acton observed, "Power tends to corrupt and absolute power corrupts absolutely. Great men are almost always bad men."[1]

2. To Know Good and Evil

Much injustice is done in the name of seeking good. Unfortunately, those in power often see things differently than those who are weak or poor. What seems to be good to those in power can actually be evil for those who are more vulnerable. This is why we humans, and especially those of us with more power and privilege, need to humble ourselves and acknowledge that only God, and not fallen human beings, can truly define what is right and wrong. Our sin-tainted ideals of righteousness and unrighteousness can steer us off into some very dark and selfish places, resulting in injustice. After all, how many acts of war or terror have been committed in the name of God against those who were deemed evil? History reveals many instances in which great evil was justified in the name of doing what was perceived as right. Our world is deeply scarred by the suffering that resulted from apartheid, bombings in Northern Ireland, the Rwandan genocide, and many other evil acts that have been committed by people who believed themselves to be doing right.

I (Colin) have a friend who is a chief of an Indigenous community on a reserve in Alberta, Canada. When I visited his community, I was haunted by what I saw. In the middle of the reserve stands an old residential school that has been abandoned for many years, but it was once one of the biggest government-funded boarding schools in all of Canada. For over eighty years, it housed Indigenous children who were ripped away from their families at the age of seven and forced by the government of Canada to be taught the white way of life in order to free them from their so-called uncivil traditions and culture. In over one hundred years of Canadian residential schooling, over 150,000 Indigenous children were forcibly taken away from their families and placed in similar schools. Any parents who tried to stop their children from being taken were arrested. In the front of the school in my friend's community is a cemetery filled with children who died while they were students there. Each little gravesite cries out against the systemic injustice of racism that these victims encountered through government-funded residential schooling. Many children who are buried in this cemetery died as the result of suicide or from freezing to death as they tried to escape the horrors of sexual, emotional, and physical abuse that ran rampant in their school. Others died from diseases that attacked their bodies, made weary by the forced labor they had to undertake at the schools.

The *Globe and Mail* reported on Truth and Reconciliation Commission hearings held in 2013 to address these abuses. In her testimony to the commission, Laurelle White, who was a member of the last of four generations to be sent to a residential school, cried as she questioned why her culture had been attacked. She asked, "What did we do other than be brown, other than have a different tradition, a different culture, have a different outlook on life? . . . What did we do that was so wrong—that they could hate us so much, to the point of death, to the point of wanting to beat the heck out of us, to get rid of us? To deny us?"[2]

The oppression of Indigenous peoples in North America was deemed justifiable by those in positions of power. According to North American colonizers, Indigenous people were savages and it was acceptable to abuse them in order to educate them in the "superior" ways of white people. Sadly, the ripple effect of these abuses continues to this day. Ongoing racial discrimination, poverty, suicide, mental health problems, and criminal victimization continue to impact Indigenous communities. And Indigenous communities are not alone in experiencing the impact of abuses. The roots of the abuse of Eurocentric power run deep within the very bedrock of North America. Systemic racism is imbedded in our political structures, causing many people to suffer. Yet each and every one of these injustices has been justified by a group of people claiming that their actions were the right thing to do. These types of excuses continue today and only go to show that as a human race, we cannot act as our own gods and apart from God cannot be trusted to know right and wrong!

3. To Pursue What Is Pleasing to the Eye

Evil often flourishes when we seek things that are pleasing to our eyes, even if it means oppressing other people or destroying our environment to get them. Like the quest for the ring in *The Lord of the Rings*, the constant pursuit of excessive wealth and consumerism often has a devastating effect. We can destroy ourselves and others in the pursuit of things "pleasing to the eye."

4. To Desire to Gain Wisdom

Humanity's desire to gain advantage over others often results in great injustices that harm the dignity of others. In the case of Adam and Eve, this desire for advantage is reflected in their desire to gain wisdom. A similar drive to gain an advantage led colonists to behave in murderous ways toward Indigenous peoples. Modern-day colonizers behave in similar ways, leaving a path of economic, environmental, and human destruction everywhere they go.

Let's admit it, we all are tempted to act like Adam and Eve, choosing to ignore God's definition of good and evil in order to create our own rules. Each of us wrestles with the desire to acquire things that are pleasing to our eyes, dismissing the fact that what we do might hurt others. A constant bombardment of consumeristic advertising feeds our material passions. And who among us isn't drawn to gain an edge over others by taking advantage of whatever opportunities come our way? In these ways, we are all tempted to participate in the sins our ancestors committed. In fact, our cultural milieu supports and even encourages such behavior. Our culture creates winners and losers who are often ranked in accordance to how close they can come to reaching godlike status through living life their own way and owning lots of possessions without worrying about the repercussions. In our voyeuristic, reality-television culture, celebrities are worshiped because of what they get for themselves, not because of what they give or do to help others.

When we believe that putting ourselves first is most important in life, we cannot avoid participating in injustice. Living a life in which we put ourselves first means that other people and our environment must come second, and often this means we manipulate others in order to achieve or maintain what we desire.

Roman Catholic social teaching, drawing on the history of Israel in the Old Testament, can teach us a lot about how these temptations unjustly impact our world.[3] The flywheel diagram on the next page reveals the ways that injustice slowly spreads within a culture

This slow progression is evident in the Old Testament accounts of the rise and fall of Israel, which depicts Israel as repeatedly abandoning the worship of the one true God in favor of **Baal,** the fertility god of Canaan. Baal represents the false gods that we create in our own image to justify behavior that puts ourselves first and that results in deepening injustice. In the cycle of Baal, we see how a society can turn on itself when it embraces the four temptations that Adam and Eve faced.

We choose to become our own gods.

We decide what is good or evil and justify our decisions in relation only to what benefits ourselves, even at the expense of others.

We chase after and accumulate possessions even if it harms other people.

We seek to take advantage over people for our own good and not for the common good of all.

As you study this diagram, ask yourself the following questions: Where do you think our society is currently headed in the cycle of Baal below? Where do you see yourself in the cycle of Baal?

The cycle of Baal in the Old Testament

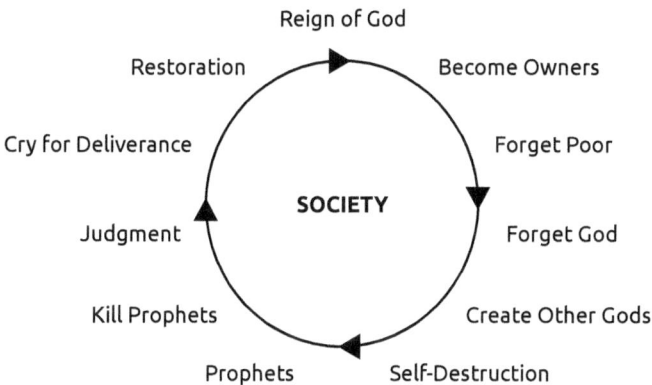

```
                        Reign of God
        Restoration         →           Become Owners

Cry for Deliverance                              Forget Poor

                          SOCIETY
  Judgment        ↑                    ↓          Forget God

    Kill Prophets                          Create Other Gods

            Prophets    ←    Self-Destruction
```

The origin and foundation for justice is found in God. However, as we benefit from life under the reign of God, we often slowly seek to become owners, claiming God's blessings as our own possessions. We do so at the expense of others, creating injustice and poverty. Then we forget the poor, whose suffering has resulted from our selfishness. In order to justify our possessions and our unwillingness to share with the poor, we forget God as the rightful owner of everything. Possessions become idols and we create other gods out of what we own. This drive for private gain and material success eventually leads to personal and societal self-destruction. However, the God of grace sends prophets to warn us about our injustice toward the poor and oppressed. Unfortunately, God's people ignore prophetic warnings by imprisoning or killing the prophets. As a result, God's judgment falls upon the self-indulgent society. This judgment eventually causes the people to cry out for God's deliverance. God brings about the restoration of God's people as they repent and return to God and life under the reign of God.

3

What Justice Looks Like

Much of Western culture is built on ancient Greek thought, which has benefited our society in many ways. However, one problematic way that the Greeks influenced the church is in a division between what the church considers sacred and secular.

Some ancient Greeks, called the **Gnostics**, adopted a worldview in which the spiritual realm of life was more important than the earthly secular realm of life. Gnostics didn't value the physical body and present living conditions of a person as equally important to the spiritual life of that person. In fact, they believed the body was a prison for the spirit. Thus, the great goal for the Gnostics was to discard the body so that the spirit could be released. This division of secular from sacred, and valuing of the spiritual over the physical, trickled into the church. It is one reason that some Christians struggle with justice-oriented action. As a result of this gnostic influence, many Christians believe that the present quality of people's lives—including their rights, education, and economic realities—is a secular matter and thus less significant than spiritual concerns. Those us who have been shaped by these views often believe that what really matters is a person's spiritual condition. This has resulted in prioritizing religious activity aimed at getting people into the church so they can experience spiritual transformation, even at the expense of meeting their physical needs. As people suffer and systems of government and social orders continue to oppress people, too many Christians have been focused solely on heaven and caring for people's spiritual well-being, and we have failed to have enough concern for their social well-being.

The Bible presents a different worldview than that of the Greek Gnostics. In ancient Hebrew thought, no division exists between sacred and secular or the spiritual and the earthly. The idea that some parts of life are more important than others was foreign to this worldview, which saw all of life as integrated. For the ancient Hebrews, all aspects of life were sacred, from the way people transact business, to how animals are treated, to laws protecting the poor. In the Old Testament, **Yahweh** (the personal God who cares about people) was concerned about all aspects of human life.

JUSTICE CREATES AND SUSTAINS SHALOM

The Hebrew word that best encapsulates this Jewish integration of all things as sacred is *shalom*. Shalom is mentioned over four hundred times in the Old Testament and provides the background for the Lord's Prayer. When Jesus prayed, "Your kingdom come, your will be done, on earth as it is in heaven" (Matthew 6:10), he was asking for the reign of God on earth, which provides for the shalom of all creation. Shalom means wholeness, unity, harmony, prosperity, and fulfillment for all people right here and now, not just in some future spiritual realm. In many ways, shalom is what God declared over creation in Genesis 1, when God said that it was "very good."

A good example of the scope of shalom is found in 2 Kings 4. In verses 8-20, we read about a childless Shunammite woman who, through the prayer of the prophet Elisha, miraculously got pregnant and gave birth to a baby boy. However, as the child grew up, he got sick and died. In a state of desperation, this bereaved mother quickly pursued Elisha to ask him to perform a second miracle and raise her child from the dead.

Upon reaching Elisha's servant we read that she

> set out and came to the man of God at Mount Carmel.
>
> When he saw her in the distance, the man of God said to his servant Gehazi, "Look! There's the Shunammite! Run to meet her and ask her, 'Are you all right [shalom]? Is your husband all right [shalom]? Is your child all right [shalom]?'"
>
> "Everything is all right [shalom]," she said. (2 Kings 4:25-26)

Initially, this woman was not telling Elisha's servant the truth—everything was not all right! But just a few verses later we read that she did tell Elisha the truth about her son who had died. In response to her words, Elisha brings her son back to life (2 Kings 4:35).

In this story we have a beautiful and practical picture of what shalom looks like. In the two verses quoted above, the phrase "all right" is mentioned four times concerning the condition of the Shunammite's family. The words translated "all right" are actually *shalom* in the original Hebrew. What we see here is a great concern for the practical well-being of people.

Are you shalom? Is your husband shalom? Is your child shalom? She responds, "Everything is shalom."

The lesson is that God is very concerned about the shalom
of all people. This goes back to God's original creation purpose
described in Genesis 1. God wants everyone and everything to
experience life as "very good." God wants all people, not just
some, to live in a state of shalom, which includes having a roof
over their heads, healthy bodies, and emotional and spiritual
well-being. In the words of this woman, God wants everything
to be shalom, not just people's spiritual well-being.

Later on, we read about this woman once again. Appar-
ently, she had to leave her home in Shunem for seven years
because of a famine that had overtaken the land. During that
time, she became a widow. Upon her return, she appeals to the
king to get her house and land back. Gehazi, Elisha's servant,
vouches for this woman, and we read that the king "assigned
an official to her case and said to him, 'Give back everything
that belonged to her, including all the income from her land
from the day she left the country until now'" (2 Kings 8:6).

Once again, we see God's Genesis 1 concern for shalom
in action as this woman comes back to her hometown. She
returns broke and husbandless, and she is in great need of
justice in order to reclaim the house and land that are right-
fully hers. This is only right and is necessary in order for
her to live in shalom. In response to her condition, the king
gives back everything that belonged to her, including her
land, income, and her home to live in. This is shalom, made
possible by justice, and it came about through the politically
powerful using their authority in a just way, as opposed to an
unjust manner that would have ignored this woman's needs.
The actions of this king are a perfect example of how doing
justice creates and sustains shalom by making sure that people

have what they need to flourish in all the spiritual, physical, social, and emotional aspects of their lives.

As you can see from the story of this woman, God is not simply concerned with the souls of people at the expense of their physical well-being. That would be unjust. Rather, God is also concerned that people have the opportunity to develop into the fullness of their humanity. This includes the physical, emotional, intellectual, and spiritual aspects of all people. When we strive to provide this type of shalom for all people, we are doing justice.

Living out God's justice allows for the shalom of all people equally, including those who lack power such as this displaced widow. In order to manifest justice on earth as it is in heaven, we must be engaged in social action as well as preaching. Just as Jesus demonstrated the kingdom of God on earth as a community characterized by shalom—wholeness, health, and completeness—so we too must do the same in our actions and in our prayers.

When looking at our world today, those who seek shalom-like justice must ask these important questions based on the Lord's Prayer: What would God's shalom-like kingdom look like on earth as it is in heaven? How can we join God in bringing justice to fulfill God's will for shalom right here now on earth as it is in heaven?

When we ask these two questions, we are forced to acknowledge that it is a great injustice for anyone to lack what is needed to live in shalom. For example, in God's kingdom, children do not go to school hungry. They are not abused. They do not live in poverty. God's will is not to have a world of gross economic inequality where many go to bed on empty stomachs each night while others are ill from overconsumption. It is not God's intention for children born in some countries to be sixty times more likely to die than children born in other countries.[1] In the kingdom, frontline workers should never get laid off while company CEOs are rewarded with millions of dollars in bonuses.[2]

None of this is God's will. None of this is shalom. All of this is injustice.

THE THREE CONCERNS OF JUSTICE

When we consider shalom as a description of what justice looks like, we need to realize that in order to be people who live shalom-like justice, we need to be concerned about several aspects of life.

1. Concerned about the Shalom of Our Communities

As we have seen, Jesus' central teaching in the Gospels was built around this concept of the kingdom coming now. In the Gospels, the kingdom is mentioned more than one hundred times. For Jesus, the reign of God is characterized by justice for all, as seen in the shalom he brought. Jesus modeled and proclaimed shalom in all he did and said in his life and ministry. We too must do the same.

2. Concerned about Life before Death as Well as Life after Death

As Old Testament Hebrew thought teaches us, God is not simply concerned with the spiritual state of people; he is also concerned that people have the opportunity to develop into the fullness of their humanity. This includes the physical, emotional, and intellectual aspects of all people.

3. Concerned about the Spirituality of People as It Directly Affects Their Physical, Emotional, and Intellectual Health

Humans consist of a holistic integration of spiritual, physical, emotional, and intellectual components. These components work together, influencing each part toward health or illness. This is why we cannot emphasize one over the other. To do so risks perpetuating injustice. For example, it is difficult to focus on your relationship with Jesus (spiritual and emotional) if you have no food in your stomach (physical). It is a challenge to expand one's knowledge of God (intellectual/spiritual) if one cannot read (intellectual). It is difficult to develop a healthy image of God and to trust God as a parent (emotional) if you have deep psychological scars from the past (emotional/physical). True spirituality involves the integration and wholeness of all aspects of a person's being.

LIVING IT OUT: CREATING AWARENESS OF SHALOM

In my younger years, I (Judith) served as director at an urban drop-in center. We hosted a basketball program that started around dinnertime and most of the young people who attended hadn't eaten when they arrived. Their physical hunger, accompanied by their excitement for the game, often bred frustration and anger.

As the basketball drop-in sessions gained momentum, more young men came and brought their girlfriends and little children. As a result, the whole landscape of our basketball program changed in a matter of weeks. Everyone who came felt welcomed by our volunteer team and we all fell in love with one another. We started getting to know each person who entered our doors by name, and in time we began to understand the needs of the greater community.

As the numbers grew, so did our programming. Soon we had a nutrition program, a toddler program, a program for job seekers, and a counseling program. The drop-in center became a home where families felt welcome and tummies were fed, and frequently souls were healed and filled before the participants walked out to face their respective challenges. Our program became a holy place where these young men came with their families each week. This became their shalom community, and as the relationships grew, so did the space for deep and vulnerable spiritual conversations. Those of us who were present shared a unique language, one that was culturally relevant and that fit the world from which these young people came. Jesus became real to them because those who welcomed them into this space considered the holistic needs of each individual. Their physical, spiritual, and mental well-being were tended to. We experienced the shalom of our community on those nights. Something incredibly sacred happened and we all saw and felt it.

I also recall some of the saddest moments from my time there. One year, we hosted a Christmas dinner, perhaps one of the first Christmas dinners that some had ever experienced. Right after we said grace over the food, some of the boys literally jumped to the table, filling the pockets of their coats with fistfuls of food while piling more food onto their plates as high as they could. One of our volunteers felt compelled to try to set some of them straight, and told them that they were ill-mannered. We were stunned by one boy's response. He said, "Sir, I'm sorry. I don't ever eat at my house and I just don't know when I'll be able to eat again. I'm just really hungry."

Another situation I recall occurred when Darian, one of the young men we knew through the drop-in center, was shot. We knew at some point we would likely be asked to respond to a situation like this, but this was the first time. We visited Darian in the hospital. We were so green in ministry that we didn't yet know how to deal with this situation. We quickly went to the hospital, Bible in hand, ready to share the Word of God with Darian. Something about this approach felt off, but we felt compelled to share some Scripture and a prayer with him. Doing so felt urgent and necessary to us. Darian's response broke our heart. In pain, and with what little energy he had, he said, "I'm not ready to hear all that, man. But I have a question for you. Is it wrong to steal food if you're hungry?"

4

God's Restoration Plan

Why did Jesus come to earth? Be careful how you answer this question because your answer will reveal how well you understand shalom-like justice.

Some Christians would answer this question as follows: "Jesus came to earth to die for our sins so we can get to heaven."

This answer discloses a gnostic view of Jesus' mission. It is strictly a spiritual understanding of the mission of Jesus as a personal salvific event: "Jesus came to die for me so I can be with him in paradise one day." This answer makes the spiritual implications of the death and resurrection of Jesus paramount, at the expense of Jesus' commitment to the practical well-being of people.

Other Christians would answer this question by saying, "Jesus came to earth to show us how we ought to live our lives." This answer also demonstrates a limited understanding of Jesus' life and mission, one that sees life as purely secular, only concerned with people's physical, emotional, and social well-being, at the expense of their spiritual needs.

In both answers, we see divides among the spiritual, physical, emotional, and social aspects of human life. Each answer places value on either the secular or the sacred at the expense of the other. Truth be told, the answer is not either/or; it is both/and.

One of the most enlightening experiences I (Colin) ever had occurred when I read all four gospels together. While reading the gospels in this manner, it became very clear to me that the reason Jesus came to earth was to tear down the walls of separation between humanity and God and between fellow humans. This great divide impacts everything, including the physical, emotional, spiritual, and social aspects of humanity. In the Gospels it becomes very evident that, like the Hebrews of old, Jesus saw everything as sacred. There was no secular/sacred divide for Jesus, and his life and mission reflected this view of reality.

In Matthew 6:25-34, Jesus is teaching about the concerns people have for their day-to-day lives. He encourages his listeners not to worry about their legitimate needs for food, clothing, and health, which were all issues of great concern in his day for those who longed for God's shalom. Instead, Jesus goes to the root of the issue by saying, "Seek first his kingdom and his righteousness, and all these things will be given to you as well" (Matthew 6:33).

The word *righteousness* in this verse (and in most other verses when the word *righteous/righteousness* shows up in the New Testament) really means "justice" in the original Greek. So according to Jesus, if we seek the kingdom of God, doing so must also involve seeking God's justice. There is no separation between the spiritual (kingdom of God) and the secular (justice/righteousness). They are all one and the same. And, if we see the kingdom of God in this light, it means that seeking God's justice together fosters a community where the basic needs of all, such as food and clothing, will be met. This is why Jesus says, "All these things will be given to you as well" (Matthew 6:33).

Jesus and God's kingdom embody justice. Throughout the Gospels, we also see Jesus active in spiritual activities—attending synagogue, participating in religious rituals, preaching, teaching, and praying. At the same time, we see Jesus deeply engaged in the physical, emotional, and social concerns of those around him—caring for the poor and the oppressed, healing the sick, speaking up for the forgotten, confronting unjust systems, and challenging abusive leaders. In this way, Jesus' life encompassed holistic concerns. He cared for spiritual needs as well as physical needs, not at the expense of one over the other. Jesus understood the importance of sustaining a healthy interconnectedness of the spiritual, physical, emotional, and social dimensions of life. In this way, justice provides for the healthy flourishing of a whole community in each of these aspects of life.

Life as Jesus intended

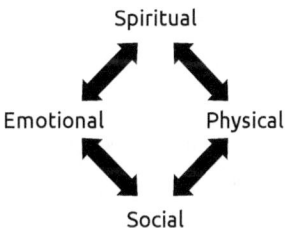

Spiritual

Emotional   Physical

Social

For Jesus, all of life is sacred and includes a holistic integration that connects spiritual, physical, social, and emotional well-being. Justice allows for the flourishing of all aspects of human life for all people.

Since all of life is sacred to God, anything that demeans a person spiritually, physically, socially, or emotionally is a sin of injustice. Injustice is an assault on the sacredness of humanity and God. Injustice throws a wrench into the shalom of God's kingdom by creating harmful divisions between God and humanity as well as between people. Jesus came to tear the walls of division down in order to restore the sacredness of all of life.

Life as Jesus intended

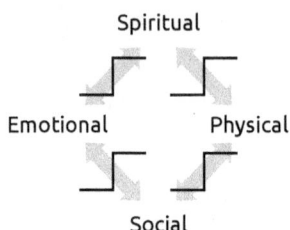

Spiritual

Emotional Physical

Social

Injustice takes place whenever division occurs between the spiritual, physical, social, and emotional well-being of people.

We see Jesus fighting injustice by addressing the various divisions in the spiritual, physical, social, and emotional well-being of people in the Gospels.

- Jesus touches and heals lepers. By doing this, Jesus tears down the wall of separation that results from the view in his day that lepers, or any other people for that matter, were considered unclean and banned from worship in the temple as unacceptable to God.
- Jesus welcomes tax collectors and sinners. By doing this, Jesus tears down the wall of separation between the religious community and people who were labeled sinners.
- Jesus befriends Samaritans and women labeled as sinful. By doing this, Jesus tears down the wall of separation between cultures and genders.
- Jesus was born into poverty and oppression.[1] Through the incarnation, Jesus lives as one who is poor and oppressed, and draws on his own life experience to tear

down the walls of division between the rich and the poor, and between the powerful and the powerless.

- Jesus stands up against unjust systems and unjust leaders, which eventually lead to his execution. By doing this, Jesus attacks the very structures that cause division in the first place.

Each of Jesus' actions for social justice has physical, social, emotional, or religious ramifications. For example, lepers were physically ill, emotionally abandoned, and socially rejected because of their disease. They also suffered spiritually because they were viewed as being unclean and cursed by God and were not permitted to worship at the temple. Jesus broke down all of these divisions that unjustly impacted lepers by touching and healing them. We also see how three of these divisive realities impacted Samaritans. **Samaritans** were socially rejected as inferior to the people of Israel, which resulted in emotional suffering. Yet Jesus accepted Samaritans and raised them onto equal footing with the Jews who hated them.

Wherever and whenever sin divides the sacred worth of human beings, we see Jesus tearing down the walls of divisiveness that produced terrible injustices. As a result, Jesus often found himself in trouble with authorities as he broke the religious rules that perpetuated such divisive injustice. From Jesus, we learn that living justly often involves breaking societal norms or even laws. Scripture tells us that Jesus not only heals lepers, but he touches them, breaking religious and social rules by tearing down barriers between people groups. Jesus doesn't just talk to sinners, but he eats with them, once again breaking social and cultural rules by becoming known as a friend of sinners. Without embarrassment, Jesus gladly accepts the love he receives from a woman "who lived a sinful life" when she pours perfume on him. By doing this, he tears down more barriers that separate this woman from others. Even in his teaching, Jesus goes out of his way to tear down barriers by highlighting Samaritans as examples of godly people and treating Gentiles as people valued by God. Jesus attacks all forms of racial, gender, economic, class, and even environmental barriers that cause division spiritually, physically, socially, and emotionally and that create injustice by desecrating the sacredness of life.

In God's restoration plan, Jesus came to earth to bring justice by tearing down the walls of division separating people from God and from one another. With this in mind, we can also see our role as members of the church. In Matthew 16:18-19 Jesus said, "And I tell you that you are Peter, and on this rock I will build my church, and the gates of Hades will not overcome it. I will give you the keys of the kingdom of heaven; whatever you bind on earth will be bound in heaven, and whatever you loose on earth will be loosed in heaven."

Jesus' purpose for the church was to take an offensive stance toward the gates of hell. Gates are used to keep people out, and Jesus reminds us that his church is to tear down the gates of hell wherever they may be. According to Jesus, the church is to be active and effective in taking on any unjust oppressive power that can create hell in our world. Gates, like walls, are used to separate people, and they must be torn down. Interestingly, Jesus also gives us the keys of the kingdom of heaven. These keys represent access to the kingdom of God, in which we can open the doors of shalom-like justice here on earth.

LIVING IT OUT

Shalom-like justice is meant to invite others in so we can reflect together the unity of the Trinity. Tearing down the walls of injustice and creating a culture of restoration is meant to be done together, not alone. We all have unique contributions in responding to injustice. We need unity, especially if we intend to lean into a life of restoring shalom to individuals and our community. There are plenty of reasons why we should choose community on our justice journey. Through community we can contribute to the work of an organization whose members are already experts at restoring justice. We don't have to create a launching pad ourselves because other people have already established many organizations where we can contribute our time and passion. Community also gives us inspiration, as well as growth and sustainability for the long run. Community can even give us incredible resources to share with those we are serving.

If we are to work in community with others, we must become people of peace and seek out people of peace. This is a priority for pursuing justice. But what does it truly mean to be a person of peace in a community context? People of peace are individuals who are welcoming to the followers of Jesus and serve as much-needed partners in doing the justice work to which we are called. People of peace provide a gateway to relationships in a neighborhood, a community, or a family. In the New Testament we see some of those whom many looked down on because of their position in life as important people of peace. Lydia, the Ethiopian eunuch, the Samaritan woman, and the centurion are all people of peace, though many of them were despised because of their backgrounds.

People of peace may be people whose race, socioeconomic status, or life experience differs from our own. I (Judith) recall the diversity of the wonderful individuals who served as people of peace for me when I entered unknown communities. Many of those people became my friends. Sharon is one of them. We used to call her our "walking phone book." She was an awkward middle school student who knew all the children in her school, where they lived, and their phone numbers. Everyone knew Sharon, and when asked how they found out about our youth drop-in program, many people would mention her. Without knowing it, Sharon was a catalyst for connecting us to that community. Each part, each person, each gift, is important for working together to bring justice to people's lives. Justice is not just personal; it is interpersonal. We need our community, our faith in God, and those who are the receivers of restorative shalom.

Let us value doing justice together. Look for people of all backgrounds who welcome you, receive you, are open to you, and are interested in the life you live as a follower of Jesus. In those relationships, the Spirit is moving and a divine friendship is being created. Be interested in other people's lives as well. The ***imago Dei***, or image of God, lives lives in them. Together, you can assist and serve one another. Be intentional as you pray for and seek people of peace. We need each other and God wants to provide community for all of us so that we can continue to be healthy in God's incredible plan of restoring individuals and communities together.

5

The Eight Traits of Justice

In the Old Testament, we encounter the Hebrew God, Yahweh (often translated as "LORD" in our English Bibles). Yahweh's compassion makes God completely different from all the other gods worshiped in the ancient Near East. These gods were violent, angry deities who enjoyed punishing people for no apparent reason and who had no concern for the state of humanity. However, Yahweh is different. Yahweh is portrayed as possessing great compassion and concern for the poor and oppressed. The Scripture says, "Yet the LORD longs to be gracious to you; therefore he will rise up to show you compassion. For the LORD is a God of justice. Blessed are all who wait for him!" (Isaiah 30:18).

Yahweh hears and feels for people who suffer. God is moved by the plight of the Hebrews enslaved in Egypt. In Exodus, God says, "I have indeed seen the misery of my people in Egypt. I have heard them crying out because of their slave drivers, and I am concerned about their suffering" (Exodus 3:7).

Yahweh even has compassion on animals, as seen in a response to the citizens of Nineveh. God tells Jonah: "Should I not have concern for the great city of Nineveh, in which there are more than a hundred and twenty thousand people who cannot tell their right hand from their left—and also many animals?" (Jonah 4:11)

Throughout Scripture, Yahweh is seen as "a father to the fatherless, a defender of widows, is God in his holy dwelling. God sets the lonely in families, he leads out the prisoners with singing; but the rebellious live in a sun-scorched land" (Psalm 68:5-6).

Yahweh opposes those who cause great injustice toward others. When this happens, Yahweh confronts those who do injustice as a protector of those who suffer.

WHY JUSTICE IS SO IMPORTANT TO GOD

For Yahweh, justice is a priority. Yet the questions must be asked: Why is justice so important to Yahweh? Why does God care so much for the orphan and the widow, the poor and the oppressed? In order to answer these questions, we need to understand the origin of the name God uses to describe himself and to understand the meaning of the kingdom of God.

1. God Embodies Justice: The Meaning of Yahweh

The meaning of the name "Yahweh" is closely associated with Moses's calling from God to free the Israelites from the injustice of slavery (Exodus 3). When Moses asked God what name he should use to describe God to the enslaved people of Israel, we read that "God said to Moses, "I AM WHO I AM. This is what you are to say to the Israelites: 'I AM has sent me to you'" (Exodus 3:14).

In this way, Yahweh's name is forever tied, through the exodus event, with salvation and liberation. By describing himself as "I AM" (Yahweh), God reveals that he is always present to those who experience injustice and is actively involved in the human struggle.

2. Justice Represents the Kingdom of God

Justice can also be seen as representing the kingdom of God. Like any kingdom, God's kingdom has rules, and it is plain from Scripture that justice is the number one rule in the kingdom of God. This is why the Old Testament consistently describes the kingdom of God in terms of justice for the poor and oppressed. It is also why we see the prophets constantly calling the Israelites back to repentance when they oppress and mistreat the poor. A good example of this is seen in the words of the prophet Micah, who describes God's standard for life in his kingdom when he says, "He has shown you, O mortal, what is good. And what does the LORD require of you? To act justly and to love mercy and to walk humbly with your God" (Micah 6:8).

As theologian Walter Brueggemann says, "In biblical faith, the doing of justice is the primary expectation of Yahweh."[1]

Since the kingdom of God is to be recognized by its justice, anything that is unjust must be from another kingdom, the kingdom of Satan. This kingdom of darkness, as the Bible describes it (Colossians 1:13), stands in opposition to justice and was the reason Jesus came "to destroy the devil's work" (1 John 3:8). Jesus also gave his mandate to the church to storm the gates of the kingdom of hell and destroy everything that oppresses and hurts people (Matthew 16:18). Our ability to secure victory over injustice is given to us through possessing the keys to the kingdom of God, which allows us access to God's kingdom power to overcome the kingdom of darkness.[2]

THE EIGHT TRAITS OF JUSTICE THAT MAKE THE SHALOM OF GOD'S KINGDOM VISIBLE

As we have discovered, the presence of Yahweh's shalom is a sign of justice. God's kingdom is a kingdom marked by shalom for all people, not just some. We have also seen how justice is a pivotal concern for Yahweh. Wherever there is a lack of shalom, you will find grave injustice. When this happens God's kingdom of justice must overcome the kingdom of darkness that is manifested through injustice. This is why God's people must get involved with God's righteousness here "on earth as it is in heaven."

Let's consider once again what our Roman Catholic brothers and sisters teach us about social justice by looking at eight key traits of justice that can be seen as evidence of shalom and the kingdom of God among us. This will help us identify where God's justice is lacking so we can roll up our sleeves and use God's kingdom power to work for shalom wherever it is needed.

1. The Dignity of the Human Person (Genesis 1:27, 31; Psalm 139:13-16; Ephesians 2:10)

We need to understand and uphold the sacredness of all people, regardless of whether their behavior is good or bad. The worth and value of every person is reflected in the fact that God created all humans in the image of God. Theologians call this the *imago Dei*, the image of God in all humanity. Therefore, humans are to be valued over material possessions. It is this dignity of humanity that is the foundation of a moral vision for a society of shalom. Anything that deforms the humanity of a person is injustice. This is also why we must oppose all acts that are an affront to human life. Abortion, war, the death penalty, racism, discrimination, sexism, torture, poverty, genocide, euthanasia, greed, and other policies that hurt people are all forms of injustice because they rob people of their sacred value and scar the *imago Dei* of humanity.

2. The Common Good (Genesis 2:18; 4:9; Exodus 20:1-17; Luke 10:23-37)

God has created us as social creatures, and as such we are a community that is to function for the common good of all people, not just for the good of some people. This means we must look out for others ahead of pursuing our own desires. Everything and everyone are interconnected, so if one of us hurts or takes hurtful actions, it will affect us all. As Father Gregory Boyle, founder and director of Homeboy Industries, a nonprofit serving gang members in Los Angeles, says, "The wrong idea has taken root in the world. And the idea is this: There just might be some lives out there that matter less than other lives."[3]

Seeking the common good is a trait of those who live for the kingdom of God. It has many implications in our lives. It means that what happens on a reservation for Indigenous people or in a poor rural or urban community needs to be a concern for those who live in wealthier suburbs or cities because we are called to seek the common good of all people. Living for the common good of all people means that economic profit and personal gain should never come at the expense of others or our environment. If we do not live for the common good of all, we will end up committing many injustices.

3. The Preferential Option for the Poor (Deuteronomy 15:1-2, 4-5, 7-18; Matthew 25:31-46; Luke 4:18-19; James 1:26-27)

It has been said that our basic moral test as a society can be seen in the way that we treat the poor and most vulnerable among us. The poor and weak have the most urgent moral claim on the conscience of our nation. We are called to look at our politics, decision-making, and choices based on how they affect vulnerable people. We must put the needs of the poor and powerless first and foremost.

4. The Promotion of Peace and Disarmament (Micah 4:3; Matthew 5:38-48; Luke 15:11-24; Acts 17:22-29)

We are one human family and God is the Father of all of us. For this reason, acts of violence are a great affront to God and those God loves. In Matthew 5:38-48, Jesus teaches the importance of nonviolence as a way of combatting social injustice. In this passage Jesus shares three shalom-like responses to injustice that respect the dignity of both the oppressed and the oppressor. Jesus says:

> You have heard that it was said, "Eye for eye, and tooth for tooth." But I tell you, do not resist an evil person. If anyone slaps you on the right cheek, turn to them the other cheek also. And if anyone wants to sue you and take your shirt, hand over your coat as well. If anyone forces you to go one mile, go with them two miles. Give to the one who asks you, and do not turn away from the one who wants to borrow from you. "You have heard that it was said, "Love your neighbor and hate your enemy." But I tell you, love your enemies and pray for those who persecute you, that you may be children of your Father in heaven. (Matthew 5:38-45)

When faced with injustice from others we are to:

- Turn the other cheek when we are slapped

- Give away our coat when someone takes our shirt
- Walk an extra mile when someone forces us to walk only one mile

When reflecting on these teachings of Jesus, theologian Walter Wink claims that Jesus created a third way to respond to violence.[4]

The first response of many people to violence is to oppose it with violence. The problem with this approach is that it harms the *imago Dei* of both people. A second way people might respond to violence is by ignoring the offense and allowing violent injustice to continue unabated. The problem with this is that any form of injustice that is ignored allows for it to continue and grow. This leaves us with the question, "How does one oppose violence by not partaking in violence?" Wink proposes that Jesus took a third-way approach to violent injustice, one that respects the *imago Dei* in the oppressor and the oppressed. In this third way of Jesus, violence is met with neither violence nor complacency. For Jesus, turning the other cheek, giving away your coat, and walking the extra mile were brilliant methods of subversively opposing injustice while refusing to respond with violence, an approach that demonstrates respect for the sacredness of both oppressed and oppressor. Let's take a look at what the Jesus Way looks like in more detail.

When Jesus told his listeners to turn the other cheek, they understood this as an act of resistance. In their culture it was legal for people in positions of power to strike those of lower status. Their culture dictated that an enslaved person would be slapped with a right backhand blow on their right cheek. A backhanded slap was intended not only to hurt but to insult, humiliate, and degrade. However, if conflict arose between two noblemen, they were not allowed to slap each other with the back of their hand, but would strike their opponent's left cheek with their open right hand, an indication that they were equals. When struck on the right cheek with a backhand blow, a victim of this act of violence, by turning the other check, would force an aggressor who wanted to strike them again to use an open right hand, acknowledging the victim as an equal. Jesus' method of protest opposes violent injustice by making a statement that all are equals.

Jesus' listeners were also accustomed to being humiliated by poverty. Many had to sell their land to pay taxes and then were forced to pay rent to the rich landowner who now owned their land. In time, many became poor and were unable to pay rent, so their landlord would take them to court to make them pay what they owed. Oftentimes, this resulted in the wealthy landowner being awarded the poor renter's shirt as an assurance that he would be paid by the poor man. A poor man who handed the landowner his shirt and also chose to give away his coat would now be naked. What an embarrassment this would be to the landowner as well as the judge, standing there in front of the poor, naked man. What makes this even more powerful is that in Hebrew culture, nakedness was a great taboo for those who viewed it. So by getting naked, the poor man would expose both the unmerciful creditor and the oppressive law to embarrassment. In this strategy for social justice, the poor debtor would acknowledge the law but would be able to reveal the injustice of the economic system to its logical absurdity. You could call this naked justice.

Now we come to walking the extra mile. Going the "second mile" comes from the practice of Roman soldiers, who could require according to law that their subjects perform forced labor. Roman law stated that Roman soldiers could make Jews carry their load up to one mile but no more than this distance. For a soldier to force a person to carry his pack beyond a mile could result in severe penalties for the soldier. So why did Jesus advise those forced to carry the soldier's pack to carry it two miles? Imagine a soldier's shock when, arriving at the mile marker, the person carrying the pack declared, "I'll carry it for you another mile," and kept on walking. If he were to allow this to happen, the soldier would find himself in grave trouble with his superiors.

Jesus' teaching regarding peace and disarmament involves a creative response that does not require either violence or passive acceptance. Jesus proposes a third method of resistance that honors the *imago Dei* of the victim as well as the perpetrator without disfiguring their relationship with further violence.

5. The Stewardship of Creation (Genesis 1:26-30; Luke 12:24, 27-28; Matthew 10:29)

God created humanity to steward God's "very good" creation so that it would thrive, not die. In God's great wisdom, all of life—human, animal, and plant—is interdependent. This has great implications for how we treat the environment since it also affects our brothers and sisters all around the world. With the ever-concerning damage resulting from human pollution and its effect on global warming, we are clearly seeing that justice for humanity requires a just relationship with our environment. In a world in which rich nations profit the most from their polluting ways, we are now seeing how global warming increases flooding, hurricanes, droughts, and other forms of natural disaster that often disproportionally impact poor nations and communities.

6. Economic Justice (Isaiah 58; Jeremiah 7:3-12; 22:3-5, 15-17; Ezekiel 16:49; James 5:1-6)

To foster shalom, the economy must serve people, not the other way around. Laborers must be valued as more important than profit. All workers have a right to productive work, decent wages, and safe working conditions. Employers hold a very important role in this area as they contribute to the common good through the services or products they provide and by creating jobs that uphold the dignity and rights of workers. If we are to live in societies characterized by shalom, we must recognize that people have the right to economic initiative and private property, but within limits. No one should be allowed to amass excessive wealth while others lack the basic necessities of life.

7. Participation (Acts 2:42-47; 5:1-11)

For shalom to be present, people need to have a right and duty to participate in society, seeking together the common good and well-being of all. By listening to a diversity of people, with different cultures, experiences, economic statuses, and backgrounds, we are able to learn from and respect one another. When some people are not allowed the opportunity for fair participation in our society, we take away their dignity and deny their value as citizens. People who lack a voice will have little power to authentically engage society, and those with a voice will dominate. This can lead to all sorts of problems for a country, province, state, city, or community.

8. Rights and Responsibilities (Deuteronomy 26:12-13; Leviticus 19:9-18, 33-37)

In the kingdom of God, everyone has the right to the basic material necessities that are required to live a decent life. This means that government in civic, political, economic, and social areas of life has the moral responsibility to promote human dignity, protect human rights, and build the common good.

LIVING IT OUT

While Judith and I (Colin) traveled to do some training for missionaries who served in an impoverished city in Brazil, I saw all eight characteristics of injustice in one place. One particular evening we were invited to visit people addicted to crack cocaine in a part of a favela called Cracolândia (Crack-land in English).[5]

We traveled through sloping narrow streets until we came to a dimly lit road where the van stopped to let us out. Carrying coffee, juice, and bread, we slowly made our way past gang members who acted as lookouts. When they were satisfied that we were not members of rival gangs or police, they gave us freedom to be approached by the many drug-addicted people who hid in the darkness along the gloomy edges of the street. These gaunt, withered shadow people slowly came toward us, limping and stumbling. Many were mentally ill because of the terrible toll the drugs had taken on them. Some were covered in scabs; others were barely clothed. All of them were dirty, broken, and smelled horribly from living on the streets. As we gave out the bread, coffee, and juice, I was overwhelmed by the knowledge that these people were all precious children of God. All of them were deeply loved by God. God knew each beautiful one of them by name. God heard their cries and understood the hurt they carried. God knew what had happened to them in the past that had driven them to the streets and to the drugs they used to numb their pain. God saw each man and woman who had sold themselves for sex in order to get money to buy drugs. And here's the astounding reality of all of this pain—God loves each and every one of these hurting individuals.

While in the middle of this sea of people who were homeless, filthy, and drug addicted, I had a revelation. All of a sudden, I realized that I was on holy ground. As I extended some bread and juice to an emaciated, trembling, balding woman, I heard Jesus whisper, "This is my body that was broken for you and this cup is the new covenant in my blood, which is poured out for you. The bread you give these people is my body broken for them. The coffee and juice you serve my hurting children is my blood that was shed for them."

As I looked all around me, I saw people eating and drinking. Some were praying and others were actually laughing with my friends as we all unknowingly served the eucharist right there with the poorest of the poor. In Cracolândia, we were all loved by God. It didn't matter if we were on drugs or not. All of us were equally sinful yet equally loved by Jesus, who broke his body and shed his blood for each and every one of us. There on those filthy streets of despair I realized that God had made this abandoned part of town holy. Cracolândia was a sacred place.

6

What to Do about Systemic Injustice

On May 25, 2020, Minneapolis police responded to a complaint that George Floyd, a forty-six-year-old Black man, had used a counterfeit twenty-dollar bill at a local convenience store. During the arrest, Derek Chauvin, a white officer, forced Floyd to lay facedown in the street, and knelt on Floyd's neck for over eight minutes, resulting in Floyd's death. Three other police officers watched as Chauvin suffocated the defenseless Floyd, who repeatedly begged for his life, and did not make any attempts to stop him. One officer even argued with onlookers who, along with Floyd, were pleading for the fatal assault to stop. Despite plenty of time to intervene, none of the other officers did so. Later that night, Floyd was pronounced dead.

Let me ask you a question: Would the police have done this to a white man over an allegedly counterfeit twenty-dollar bill?

I think we all know the answer to this question. Floyd was murdered by an officer of the state because he was Black, not because he passed a fake twenty-dollar bill.

In countries formed out of colonization by Europeans, such as Canada or the United States, oppressive violence and force were used to gain power over those who were indigenous to the land. Hundreds of years later, Floyd's death from the knee of a white man on his neck is a powerful symbol of the continued injustice that takes place in order for some people to maintain a position of power and privilege over others. In North America (and in many parts of the world), power structures favor certain people over others: the rich over the poor, white people over Black, Indigenous, and people of color (BIPOC), and men over women.

When these power imbalances shape public policies, institutional practices, cultural representations, and other norms that work to reinforce them, we call this systemic injustice. These injustices are embedded in the history and structures of North America and have become the social norm. This is why it is so hard to eliminate these evils. Many of us who benefit the most from these imbalances cannot see, or refuse to acknowledge, their ugly reality. Why would we? After all, it is very difficult to give up power, especially for those of us who benefit from a system we have inherited.

Truth be told, the majority of us who benefit from systemic injustice can be ignorant of the full measure of the unearned assets we receive from our privilege. But those of us who suffer from systemic injustice are often acutely aware of the harm it does to our lives, families, and communities. Hundreds of years of unearned advantage can blind those of us with privilege to the reality that our life experience is not the norm for all people.

Racism is one pervasive form of systemic injustice in North America. Statistics reveal that great disparities exist between the life circumstances of white and Black communities in the United States.

- Black people are incarcerated at more than five times the rate of white people.[1]
- While Black people make up 13 percent of the U.S. population, they hold less than 3 percent of the wealth.[2]
- If Black people had the same mortality rate as white people, nearly 100,000 fewer Black people would die each year in the United States.[3]
- A recent study found that school districts that predominantly serve students of color received, on average, about $2,200 less in funding per student than mostly white school districts in the United States.[4]
- Black people have higher rates of diabetes, hypertension, and heart disease than other groups, and Black children have a 500 percent higher death rate from asthma compared with white children.[5]

Why such disparities? Sociologists point to interlocking and overlapping systemic racial inequities. For instance, multiple forms of racial inequity have contributed to the mass incarceration of people of color in the United States. Legal precedents set during the opening of the U.S. War on Drugs, launched in the 1980s under President Ronald Reagan, allow for policing policies such as racial profiling, stop-and-frisk, and coerced "consent" searches during pretextual traffic stops, vastly increasing police discretion to search citizens of their choosing.[6]

Under these policies, law enforcement have disproportionately targeted poor communities of color, resulting in far higher rates of arrest and conviction of Black and Latino Americans than of white Americans, despite the fact that people of all races sell and use drugs at similar rates.[7]

In the United States, nearly all criminal cases are resolved through plea deals, rather than through trials. Harsh and disproportionate sentencing laws and lack of financial resources to hire adequate legal counsel results in many of those arrested pleading guilty, regardless of guilt or innocence.[8]

The result is a racial disparity in U.S. incarceration rates of staggering proportions. Civil rights lawyer and legal scholar Michelle Alexander notes that "although the majority of drug users and dealers nationwide are white, three-fourths of all people imprisoned for drug offenses have been black or Latino."[9]

These racial disparities in arrest and conviction rates have contributed to the public perception that the typical drug user is a person of color, despite the opposite being true.[10]

Many people are unaware of the racism they have developed, but this **unconscious bias** clearly manifests itself when white people experience irrational fear when they come across a young Black man walking toward them on the street. Implicit racism results in many damaging consequences. For instance, it affects how many people of color receive job interviews and limits their opportunities to receive loans or enter the housing market.

I (Colin) will never forget the time one of my young mentees was arrested. As I watched events unfold, it was clear to me that his arrest was the result of many systemic injustices. A few months earlier, a city bus driver had made racially derogatory comments against children who were participating in an outing as part of one of our ministry programs. As the little children struggled to get on the bus, the driver accused our staff, many of whom were young Black leaders, of intention-ally holding back one child's bus ticket. The driver refused to move the bus until the staff paid the fifty-cent fee for that child. Using racist words, the driver complained, "I guess this is what I should expect from a neighborhood like this." Upon hearing his comment, my young mentee, one of the staff leading the outing, told the driver, "Just move the bus." The driver replied, "Is that a threat?" My young friend repeated, "Just move the bus." The bus driver called the police and complained of being threatened by a passenger. When the police came, they handcuffed my mentee and aggressively pushed him around in front of the children before pushing him out of the bus and into a police cruiser. On the drive to jail, the police called my mentee all sorts of racist names. Now this young man was known by the police, another victim of living in an impover-ished Black neighborhood.

A few months later the police barged into my mentee's small government housing home and arrested him in front of his mother and sisters. They charged him with selling crack, a charge that carries a potential minimum prison sentence of five years. The legal aid lawyer appointed for my mentee wanted him to plead guilty and possibly receive a lesser sentence. I knew that my mentee was innocent and that this had to be a case of mistaken identity, so I quickly called some wealthy friends to help get a better lawyer. Through my connections, I found a lawyer who would represent my friend.

After my mentee spent a year on house arrest, the hearing date arrived. We filled the courtroom with friends, pastors, and many mothers from my mentee's neighborhood. What we wit-nessed was a vindication. A court hearing that was supposed to last over two weeks was finished in two days. The judge threw out the case and called it a farce. Our lawyer tore the police's case to shreds for the lack of evidence and because they had clearly jumped to conclusions based on the earlier bus incident.

When the verdict was declared, I left that courtroom in great distress. I couldn't help but think of all the poor, the powerless, and the people of color who are profiled and arrested and who do not have the resources to afford a good lawyer. How many of them have been jailed over false arrests? How many of them have been given inordinately long prison sentences because of the lack of proper legal representation?

As you can see from these patterns of injustice, racism is not only a police reform issue. The injustice goes much deeper than that. It is a problem deeply rooted in inequitable power within systems that favor one group of people over another. Systemic injustices such as racial inequalities cannot be solved by addressing one area of reform alone, because the roots of systemic inequality have been ingrained in North American culture through many generations and pervade our structures and systems. Racism, like other forms of systemic injustice, is not a one-off issue to be solved but a result of an entire system that must be overhauled.

WHAT CAN WE DO ABOUT SYSTEMIC INJUSTICE?

As we talk about systemic injustice, we have focused on systemic racism. However, it is important to note that our current power systems also discriminate on the basis of other factors as well, including gender, class, and sexual orientation. The question is, What can we do about systemic injustice?

1. Listen to Those Most Harmed by Systemic Injustice

The first step we need to undertake to dismantle systemic injustice is to listen well to those who suffer from it. This is especially the case for those of us who benefit from the unjust system. In Exodus 3:7 God declares: "I have indeed seen the misery of my people in Egypt. I have heard them crying out because of their slave drivers, and I am concerned about their suffering."

Yahweh cares for those who suffer injustice and models how his followers must act. Our godly posture must be to take the time to see the misery, hear the cries of the oppressed, and be concerned about those who suffer from systemic injustice. Reflecting on the importance of truly listening to those who suffer, African American theologian Brenda Salter McNeil writes, "Whenever race and ethnicity become part of the equation, we make sweeping generalizations and use those stereotypes to justify our fear and our actions."[11]

She goes on to state, "I know that often the story told is tied to some agenda or purpose that's not being overtly stated. That's why it's important to learn what's really happening and to hear the story from trusted people who are living close to and being personally affected by the situations we seek to address."[12]

2. Humbly Examine Our Own Biases

While we see, listen, and empathize with those who suffer, we must also examine how we may be complicit in systemic injustice. It is important to listen to the prophetic voices of those strong leaders who suffer from systemic oppression. They are the ones who can best shine light into the souls of those of us who benefit from injustice and challenge us to see the ways we, like the Egyptians who enslaved the Israelites, may be holding people in bondage for our own benefit. Though their words might feel painful to those of us who benefit from unjust privilege, it is important to recognize that oftentimes the truth hurts, but it is necessary for healing, even when hearing it makes us uncomfortable. Truth leads to repentance and can free all of us, both those who benefit and those who suffer, from the shackles of systemic injustice, which harms both oppressed and oppressor.

One of those fiery prophetic voices is that of Anabaptist historian and civil rights activist Vincent Harding. Addressing the Mennonite World Conference in Amsterdam in 1967, Harding challenged his listeners to choose whether they would stand with the oppressed or the oppressors, declaring,

> The victims of the "Christian" West are rising, and in their midst stands the Christ of beggars, the outsider, Jesus of Nazareth. Do you see Him? Do you hear Him in the agony of their voices? Do you feel His Spirit blowing down the fortresses of safety, wealth and greed? He is there. We may hide, but He is there. . . . Let there be no mistake, *He* is with them; but where are we? Mennonites, Christians, [people] who love humanity, where are we? . . . Let us take no more the name of Christ in vain. For he is out in the midst of the flames. His way was to give up all he had. He stands among the bitter rock-throwers and the impassioned revolutionaries. . . . If we stay away from the rising beggars, we stay away from Him. For though He loved both oppressed and oppressor, He died outside the gate with the outcasts.[13]

3. Study Jesus

Jesus battled systemic injustice in his own context and models how we are to deal with it. In the Israel of Jesus' day, religious and cultural systems were rife with abuse. An example of this is seen in how the Jews held power over the Samaritans. At the same time, their cultural norms tended to place women at the bottom of the social hierarchy. Yet Jesus refused to uphold these unjust systems. In one poignant example, we see Jesus speaking with a Samaritan woman, asking her help to give him a drink from Jacob's well. What makes this encounter so countercultural is threefold:

Jesus is speaking to a Samaritan. Jews in Jesus' day were unlikely to stoop so low as to speak with Samaritans, who were hated by Jews, let alone ask them for help of any kind. Yet Jesus demolishes the cultural taboo that belittled Samaritans as inferior by talking with a Samaritan and humbly asking her for water.

Jesus is speaking to a Samaritan woman. Not only does Jesus defy systemic bias against Samaritans, but he also challenges sexism by asking this Samaritan woman for help. For Jesus to approach and speak with a woman in public is surprising. This is because some rabbis taught that Jewish men should not speak to any women in public, not even their own wives.

Jesus is speaking to a Samaritan woman many would reject because of her past. Finally, Jesus even goes deeper into dismantling systemic injustice by not only talking to a despised Samaritan who is a woman, but to one who also was most likely looked down on by others because she had had five husbands. Sadly, this woman's circumstances would have led many people to question her morality. However, in her defense, it is important to realize that in the abusive form of patriarchy present in Jesus' day, women had few rights and men could divorce their wives for any reason, leaving them destitute. Without a man's support, many women became vulnerable to predatory men. Jesus understood this injustice, and for this reason, we should not be surprised by how many women felt safe following him. It is also why we see Jesus openly accepting this woman and validating her worth by offering her salvation as a valued child of God.

In this one instance, Jesus attacks systemic injustice on four fronts by refusing to participate in the accepted racial, patriarchal, religious, and economic power structures of his day. His example reveals to us various principles we can embody if we are to be effective in freeing ourselves and others from the restrictive and abusive systems in our culture today. The biggest lesson we can learn from Jesus here is total acceptance and friendship with those who have been put down by the powers that be.

4. Take Action

Our hearts need to be softened by seeing, listening to, and empathizing with those who suffer. We also must examine and repent of our own complicity in systemic injustice by listening to prophetic voices that challenge our preconceived ideas. We must be willing and unafraid to cross unjust structural and cultural divides. And we must not only openly refuse to participate in any form of systemic injustice but must take concrete action to change systemic injustice.

Speaking at a mass meeting in Indianola, Mississippi, in 1964, community organizer and voting rights activist Fannie Lou Hamer urged fellow African Americans to take concrete action in the struggle for justice, despite the cost. "All we have to do is trust God and launch out into the deep," she proclaimed. "You can pray until you faint, but if you don't get up and try to do something, God is not going to put it in your lap."[14]

When we have listened to those who suffer, examined our own possible bias, and understand how Jesus handled injustice, we have a solid foundation on which to take action. This requires us to be willing to acknowledge how we might be complicit in systemic injustice. For those who suffer systemic injustice, anger is understandable, but as hard as it might be, anger must be channeled into bringing about justice, not revenge. Theologian and activist Ruby Sales, reflecting on the role of anger in work for justice, states: "Love is not antithetical to being outraged. Let's be very clear about that. . . . There are two kinds of anger. There's redemptive anger, and there's non-redemptive anger. . . . I think we have to begin to have a conversation that incorporates a vision of love with a vision of outrage."[15]

Jesus himself modeled righteous indignation in response to the injustices found in his society. He recognizes the fact that having enemies is a reality in our lives when he teaches us to "love your enemies and pray for those who persecute you" (Matthew 5:44). Yet Jesus tells us that, in our anger, we are not to seek revenge but love. Why is this the right response to injustice?

The answer can be found in the *imago Dei*, the image of God, present in all people. All people are sacred because they are created in God's image. This also means that all people are capable of change, and it gives us hope for a better world. To respond to injustice with revenge only perpetuates the hatred behind injustice. It blinds us to broader and better visions of how to make things right. It also harms those who participate in revenge.

This leaves us with an important question we must act upon whenever we feel anger in response to injustice: What kind of human being do I want to be? Do I want to dehumanize myself and others by seeking revenge that disfigures the *imago Dei* in myself and others? Or do I choose to bring about positive change by responding in love to others and thus also to myself? Revenge can never fuel effective change or empower a transformative justice movement. This is because vengefulness and bitterness will only replace oppression with another form of abuse.

When I think of Jesus' words about doing justice in love, I cannot help but think of the ancient martial art known as aikido. Aikido turns an opponent's power and aggression back on itself. The goal of aikido is to defend yourself while also protecting your opponent from being hurt. Justice modeled on aikido allows us to stand up against injustice by using whatever power the system affords us and turning it against itself, while also demonstrating love toward both oppressed and oppressors. This was the methodology of Jesus as well as that of Martin Luther King Jr., who had grace toward his oppressors because he saw them as victims of ingrained, generational racism. Dr. King's strategy to defeat systemic injustice is reflected in these words:

> Love has within it a redemptive power. And there is a power there that eventually transforms individuals. That's why Jesus says, "Love your enemies." Because if you hate your enemies, you have no way to redeem and to transform your enemies. But if you love your enemies, you will discover that at the very root of love is the power of redemption. You just keep loving people and keep loving them, even though they're mistreating you.[16]

Only love can transform systemic injustice into systems of righteousness for all people, and not just some. With this in mind, we can bring about systemic change in the name of loving justice in some of the following ways.

FOR THOSE WHO BENEFIT FROM UNJUST SYSTEMS

For those of us who benefit from systemic privilege, it is important to recognize this reality and use our power and privilege for justice. Sending tweets can be a positive thing, but it is not enough. We need to practice aikido by using our privilege to defeat systemic injustice. One way to do this is by using our privilege to open doors for those who may not otherwise have access to certain corridors of power. I (Colin) regularly bring BIPOC brothers and sisters with me to functions to which they would not otherwise have access. When I am invited to posh boardrooms to meet with wealthy businesspeople, I never go alone but always bring a few young BIPOC leaders with me. This is an opportunity for me to step back while those who have been kept out of these leadership situations step in and contribute in ways I can't. Many around these boardroom tables may never have taken the time to listen to people who look different from them or who might see things differently than their views, which are shaped by their privilege. These opportunities often lead to deeper discussions concerning privilege, power, and race. By doing this, I use my privilege to bring both worlds together. When this happens the powerful walls of systemic injustice begin to crumble as a result of new friendships, which allow young leaders opportunities to speak truth to power, but also to access leadership opportunities. This is how our little group of justice martial artists are able to turn systemic injustice against itself to defeat its evils. Aikido for justice works.

Diverse friendships are important if the rich and powerful are to come to know and learn from the victims of unjust systems. This is why it is so important to bridge the gap between rich and poor, white and Black, male and female. Through a diversity of friendships, those in power may begin their own transformative journey of justice with their new friends and, in turn, use their power to change the system to be fair and equitable for all people. Tweets, marches, and other forms of protest are all good, but we must go deeper. The roots of systemic injustice are found far beyond the reach of social media.

It is in the corridors of political, legal, and economic power as well as in the offices of religious organizations and medical institutions where change must take place. These are the places our protest marches must lead to.

I have seen lawyers, business owners, and even surgeons practice aikido. They use their influence to make sure the organizations they work for and support provide equal opportunities, pay, and benefits to BIPOC men and women. They push for equal representation on boards and in positions of influence. There is often a price to be paid for doing this. It means that those with more privilege have to give up some of their privilege, but they do so willingly because they have come to see the great injustice in the very system in which they participate.

FOR THOSE WHO SUFFER FROM UNJUST SYSTEMS

For those of us affected by systemic injustice, it is important to know that we are not alone. As a Jew, Jesus was also a victim of great injustice from his Roman conquerors. The Roman Empire treated its captive citizens cruelly, leading oppressed Jews to respond in one of two ways:

- Some became Zealots who fought back against the imperial power through violence. Sadly, this only led to more bloodshed and increased injustice.
- Others accepted their circumstances and refused to confront the powerful perpetrators of evil in their society. Unfortunately, this only reinforced the current injustice without hope for any type of change.

However, there is a third way we can respond to systemic injustice. Jesus and his followers fought against evil through loving defiance against any form of systemic injustice (see

"The Promotion of Peace and Disarmament" in chapter 5 to understand Jesus' strategy of dismantling systemic injustice). Jesus knew that the Zealots' form of resistance only leads to more death and oppression. He also disagreed with silence and passive acceptance in the face of systemic injustice, which only increases injustice. As slow as the way of Jesus might seem to be, it is the only method that has brought about historic change. It is a road map we can follow in bringing down forms of systemic injustice today.

Once again, I refer back to Dr. King, who had this to say to people who suffer from systemic injustice:

> There are three ways that individuals who are oppressed can deal with their oppression. One of them is to rise up against their oppressors with physical violence and corroding hatred. But oh, this isn't the way. For the danger and the weakness of this method is its futility. Violence creates many more social problems than it solves. . . . Another way is to acquiesce and to give in, to resign yourself to the oppression. . . . And so they resign themselves to the fate of oppression. . . . But that too isn't the way because noncooperation with evil is as much a moral obligation as is cooperation with good. But there is another way. And that is to organize mass nonviolent resistance based on the principle of love. . . . We must discover the power of love, the power, the redemptive power of love. And when we discover that, we will be able to make of this old world a new world. We will be able to make men better. Love is the only way. Jesus discovered that.[17]

LIVING IT OUT

Only defiant love can change systemic injustice. This happens best when those benefiting from the system become aware of its evil and join the oppressed to make changes. Prophetic voices, listening ears, and repentant hearts can come together to make things right. Together we can correct historic wrongs and open doors to surrender and share power.

I (Colin) will never forget the day the lightbulb went on for me concerning a possible solution regarding systemic racism. I was attending a Black Lives Matter rally and joined a crowd of protestors from diverse cultural backgrounds. As I looked around me at the sea of people and heard these wonderful young leaders confronting tragic experiences of racism and sharing ideas for dismantling it, I experienced great hope. Before me was a rainbow of young, energetic protestors who were unified for a just cause. Every one of us was present because of our conviction that Black lives matter.

I began to think about what unified such a large, diverse group. I realized that this generation is marked by friendships, dating relationships, and marriages of different cultures and backgrounds. My fellow protestors were truly a wonderful, diverse group of beautiful humanity. I heard speakers share that they were in mixed-race relationships or marriages, or their parents were from different backgrounds, and how this had joined their separate families, Black and white, together as one. Families that for generations were considered to be of different races were now joined together through marriage. Family get-togethers now include diverse people from both families, unified together. In this environment, love spreads between grandparents, uncles, aunts, and cousins from both sides of the cultural divide who are now one family. In this new reality, white grandparents, uncles, and aunts, some of whom hold positions of power thanks to white privilege, now go to sleep each night worried about their Black son- or daughter-in-law, Black grandchildren, or their beloved Black nephews and nieces. They now have literal skin in the game when it comes to overturning racial injustice. Police profiling and brutality toward people of color is a reality that affects their own family members. Racial discrimination in job opportunities hits close to home because it affects their own extended family. To them, Black lives matter because Black lives are now part of their family. In this wonderful environment of unified diversity, systemic injustice is seen in all its gory evil, flushed out because it affects all people, Black and white. In this unity, we have more power to destroy racism through love for one another.

What I heard and saw that day at the Black Lives Matter rally made me think how our Father God intends that this familial expression of shared love characterize our relationships with one another as the family of God. Our churches need to model the reality that God is our Father, and every human being is a beloved child of God, reflecting a beautiful kaleidoscope of precious colors that make up one human race. We as Christians cannot turn a blind eye toward any form of injustice directed at our fellow brothers and sisters, because we are all connected as children of God.

7

Justice and Societal Structures

As we can see from the life of Jesus, justice provides for the health and flourishing of the spiritual, physical, social, and emotional aspects of life for all people. This was also the plan of God throughout the Old Testament.

THREE STRUCTURES OF BIBLICAL JUSTICE

When Israel was preparing to enter the Promised Land, God set up three structures to foster justice and shalom in the land. These structures were:

1. Religious Structure (Deuteronomy 6:4-6, 14-16)

God instituted Israel's religious system to enable the people to know and love "Yahweh," the God of justice who cares for people. This religious system was designed to enable the people to always be in relationship with a God who expects justice from his people. God would not tolerate a religious system to be used for any other purpose, including to enable people to follow other gods such as power, money, consumerism, or violence.

2. Political Structure (Deuteronomy 6:17-19)

God also instituted Israel's political order to help people live life with shalom-like justice. This political system was meant to derive its power and authority from leaders who were living, both personally and corporately, in a close relationship with the God of justice, as opposed to living in a close relationship with big business or special interest groups. For God, a just political structure focuses on the prospering of all people. A political structure that helps only some people to prosper is unjust.

3. Economic Structure (Deuteronomy 6:10-13; 15:4-11)

Israel was also to have a fair economic system. In Deuteronomy 15:4, God instructed Israel that "there should be no poor among you." Impartial banking, organized sharing systems, and equitable labor practices were all an important part of Israel's practices of economic justice. The economic system was to be built on a concept seen throughout the Old Testament, that the Hebrew people own nothing because the land they are living on was given to them by God. Their wealth was not to be individually owned wealth; it was to be commonly shared. Therefore, the task of those who managed the wealth was to be good stewards of the wealth that came from God. Their responsibility was to maintain and use wealth for the common good of all of Israel, not just for part of Israel.

HOW THE STRUCTURES WORK

For Good

When these three structures work together, as they are supposed to, they are seen as follows:

The religious structure declares God's rule is supreme and that every person is equally a child of God. If we are connected to this type of religious structure, based on a Genesis 1 *imago Dei* view of humanity, then the economic structure will care for and increase the wealth for all people. The political structure would also ensure that society was practicing stewardship and equitable distribution for all, not just for the privileged few, providing justice and equitable treatment for all.

For Bad—A Case Study: Jerusalem in the Day of Ezekiel (Ezekiel 22)

When the three structures God had created to bring shalom-like justice fell apart, Jerusalem became unjust. Israel was now under the domain of the kingdom of hell.

In Ezekiel 22 we can read about the breakdown and ram-ifications of what happens when the religious, political, and economic structures God created become corrupt.

1. Political System (Ezekiel 22:6-7, 25)

In Ezekiel 22, it is clear that the political leaders' actions were not for the common good. There was no justice and equi-table treatment for all. The leaders were greedy, power hungry, and neglecting their God-given responsibility to maintain jus-tice for all.

2. Economic System (Ezekiel 22:12-13, 27, 29)

Ezekiel also condemns the economic powers that had become exploitative. Instead of maintaining the common wealth for everyone, leaders used their positions to exploit the people and make as much money as possible for themselves. They no longer saw themselves as stewards of the economy. Instead of sharing the wealth that God had given them to manage for the equal benefit of all, they took the wealth as if it were their own to handle as they saw fit. The more they accumulated wealth for themselves, the more ways they found to deprive others. This resulted in the inevitable growth in the number of people living in poverty.

3. Religious System (Ezekiel 22:26, 30)

God established priests and prophets to build and main-tain the people's relationship with God. But what did these religious leaders do with this great privilege? They broke their own relationship with God and did not teach justice and truth. They did this so that they could gain wealth and power from the political and economic leaders. The prophet condemns these religious leaders for using their power to control the peo-ple by endorsing the corrupt political and economic structures and calling them good. As a result, the people accepted the oppressive circumstances brought about by the corrupt leaders of these structures as ordained by God.

When these three structures become corrupted, they poison all of society. To counter this problem, God raises up righteous prophets to call these structures to accountability.

THE ROLE OF PROPHETS (EZEKIEL 22:1-2, 30-31)

The role of prophets was to call the power structures to account. Prophets stood outside of the establishment, neither bound to them nor economically dependent on them. It was up to the prophet to cry "Thus saith the Lord" to the people and power structures. However, what happens when the prophet himself becomes impacted by the power structures? Either the prophet's critical voice is silenced or the prophet supports the corrupt system and gives it divine sanction and legitimacy, as seen in Ezekiel 22:28.

DESTINY OF CIVILIZATIONS THAT HAVE CORRUPT STRUCTURES (EZEKIEL 22:3-5, 15-16)

When the political, economic, and religious structures are not functioning as they are supposed to, people turn on each other as the civilization enters an everybody-for-themselves survival mode. Exploited and oppressed by the systems, the people exploit and oppress each other in turn.

EVIL POWER BEHIND THE POWERS (EPHESIANS 6:12; 1 PETER 3:22)

The power structures that are systemically unjust and victimize people have an evil and a spiritual dimension. Corruption and oppression are not only a systemic problem but a spiritual problem as well. This points to the reality that spiritual, physical, emotional, and social dynamics are deeply intertwined. Spiritual forces are committed to abusing the structures to capture cities, provinces, and nations for the evil one. These three structures—political, economic, and religious, created by God to bring about shalom—are invaded by evil demonic powers sent to corrupt and destroy all that is good in the city, province, or nation. This is why it is so important for the church to function in a holistic manner in addressing the religious, economic, and political structures of our day. Our duty to participate in spiritual warfare against evil powers present in these systems calls us to abandon any selfish or gnostic underpinning that might be present in our church structures.

CONCLUSION

We have come to understand that God wants everyone to experience shalom. In God's plan, justice is an act of restoration, realigning human life with his creation purposes for the shalom for all people, not just some people. Everything is sacred in God's eyes, and he desires that religious, economic, and political structures work together for the common good. As followers of Jesus, we must be active in living and bringing a prophetic perspective to our religious, political, and economic structures so that they align themselves with God's shalom-like justice. This is the meaning of justice in the Bible.

LIVING IT OUT

As we end this exploration of the topic of justice, we want to share a final story.

When working with the urban poor, we always rely on God to provide for our needs through volunteers and financial donors. Our intention is to support communities with resources so that we can continue our work to empower local leaders from the neighborhoods we serve. To do this we recruit people to volunteer, write grants, and share our story with private donors, churches, and foundations. We also have sought support from government agencies that are set up to assist nonprofits. All of these resources are incredibly important so we can continue our important work in the housing projects we serve.

Some years ago, Colin submitted a grant proposal to a Canadian government agency, requesting funding for our Christian nonprofit to employ young leaders in after-school programs in a low-income neighborhood. We were confident that our organization met all the targets and values for this government grant. A few months later, we were asked to attend a meeting to hear if our proposal had been accepted. With great excitement, we attended this gathering, confident that we would be awarded a very generous grant to sustain our work with local young leaders. In the meeting, we were told we had met all the criteria of the grant, and the organization's leaders affirmed that our proposal was head and shoulders above all the other proposals. We had checked every box they were looking for in organizations that they sought to support. But then we were told that they could not accept us as a partner because we were a faith-based organization. Their reason for this was that they did not want to appear to be discriminatory.

What happened next was quite profound. With nothing to lose, Colin challenged the government organization, telling the leaders that they were guilty of discrimination. After all, turning us down for a grant because our work is based in our Christian faith is, in itself, very discriminatory. Colin went on to walk the foundation staff through a short history lesson of social justice and the ways that Christians stood up against slavery, led the civil rights movement, started the first hospitals, began public schools, and marched for voting rights for women. Colin then asked the organization leaders whether they would have joined Martin Luther King Jr., a Christian pastor, and the civil rights movement. They all said yes. He then asked if they would have joined William Wilberforce, a Christian politician, in his fight against slavery in England. Again, they all said yes. Colin continued, asking them if they were supportive of other current social justice initiatives such as the Salvation Army and its housing programs, Covenant House and its shelter systems, St. Joseph Hospital, World Vision, and Habitat for Humanity. They all said yes to these questions.

With nothing to lose, Colin dropped the gauntlet and challenged them. He told them that, according to their policy of not supporting faith-based charities, they would not have supported the civil rights movement under Dr. King, because of its roots in the Southern Christian Leadership Conference. Nor would they have been able to support the abolitionist movement, because Christians started faith-based movements to fight against slavery. The early public school and hospital movements would also have been rejected because many were started by Christian ministries. They couldn't even support programs that provide overnight winter shelter for people who are homeless because many of these are led by Christian organizations just like ours.

To the government leaders' credit, they called us up the next day to tell us that we were receiving the grant after all, and we were able to invest that money in many young leaders. Today, thanks to their support, we now see many of the young people we were able to help through this grant serving as wonderful leaders in their respective positions of influence in our city. This is a perfect example of how justice-focused religious organizations, accompanied by fair economic and political powers, can make a difference in the shalom of our world. In this case, there was a need for a prophetic voice to challenge political leaders to look beyond their own limited perspective and to help our city. Let us be confident in our understanding of what true justice is and, when necessary, use our prophetic voice in challenging unjust religious, economic, and political powers to do what is right in the name of justice.

Glossary

Baal: A religious idol that was worshiped through the execution and sacrifice of humans mainly in the form of innocent children.

Gnostics: A popular group of people in ancient Greece who taught that the spirituality of a person holds paramount importance over the fleshly body, which was deemed a negative obstacle to human potential.

imago Dei: The image of God found in every human being that makes a person sacred and of immense value.

justice: A state of being in which all people are equally valued and treated fairly as beings created in the image of God.

kingdom of God: A phrase Jesus used many times to describe God's reign on our earth in the form of loving justice and fairness for all people, especially for those who are most vulnerable.

Samaritans: A break-off group of Jews who lived in Samaria and who were despised by the Jewish people in Jesus' day for intermarrying with non-Jews and participating in political and religious conflict because of their differences in worshiping God.

shalom: The quality of holistic peace in which people experience material, spiritual, physical, and emotional wholeness and well-being.

systemic injustice: The oppression, devaluing, or disempowerment of certain groups of people by political, economic, or religious systems of power. Systemic injustice often comes about through unfair laws, negative profiling, and the limitation of opportunities and power based on hundreds of years of ingrained false cultural assumptions that benefit some people over others.

unconscious bias: Unfair, judgmental, or damaging beliefs that a person or system unknowingly adopts toward people or certain ways of life as being inferior.

Yahweh: The Hebrew name for the God of justice.

Discussion and Reflection Questions

CHAPTER 1

1. Do you recall the journey in which your soul said yes to Jesus and you decided to follow him? Journal about your memory of that time, and include the curiosity and excitement of that experience.

2. Think through possible justice initiatives for which your life experiences have prepared you. What is your soul saying to you about potential justice-oriented initiatives that you can participate in?

3. How can you better balance your life so that you are able to move toward a sustainable and healthy life that expresses God's intentions for your spiritual life and for justice?

CHAPTER 2

1. How does modern life tend to make us forget Yahweh? What can we do to stay connected to God?

2. Who are the prophets of our day and how can we stay connected to the prophetic voices in our society?

3. In what ways do we or our society attempt to kill or silence prophets? How can we empower and enlarge prophetic influence on ourselves and those around us?

CHAPTER 3

1. Explain why justice-oriented action is difficult for some Christians.

2. Give some illustrations from the Gospels of how Jesus created a culture of shalom in the spaces in which he moved.

3. How can you create a culture of shalom in the spaces to which you are called?

CHAPTER 4

1. How can we help bring about shalom in spiritual, physical, emotional, and social areas of life?

2. It takes great courage to take an offensive stance against the gates of hell. What opportunities do you have for being active in restorative justice? What justice issue do you feel drawn to address and how can you begin to bring about change?

CHAPTER 5

1. What do you think the world would be like if Yahweh were not compassionate?

2. In what ways have you seen the presence or absence of the eight traits of justice in your life, community, or world?

3. What are ways you can participate in God's kingdom reign?

CHAPTER 6

1. What are some things you can do to listen for, see, and feel the suffering of others?

2. What are some practical ways you can use aikido justice to bring about systemic change?

3. How can you unite with a diverse group of people to bring about systemic change?

CHAPTER 7

1. How do you see the three structures of biblical justice working together in our current cultural context for good? How have you seen them corrupted and working for evil?

2. How can you support these structures to work for good?

3. Is there a prophetic role for justice in our present culture? What is the outcome if we do not use our prophetic voices?

Shared Convictions

Mennonite World Conference, a global community of Christian churches that facilitates community between Anabaptist-related churches, offers these shared convictions that characterize Anabaptist faith. For more on Anabaptism, go to ThirdWay.com.

By the grace of God, we seek to live and proclaim the good news of reconciliation in Jesus Christ. As part of the one body of Christ at all times and places, we hold the following to be central to our belief and practice:

1. God is known to us as Father, Son and Holy Spirit, the Creator who seeks to restore fallen humanity by calling a people to be faithful in fellowship, worship, service and witness.

2. Jesus is the Son of God. Through his life and teachings, his cross and resurrection, he showed us how to be faithful disciples, redeemed the world, and offers eternal life.

3. As a church, we are a community of those whom God's Spirit calls to turn from sin, acknowledge Jesus Christ as Lord, receive baptism upon confession of faith, and follow Christ in life.

4. As a faith community, we accept the Bible as our authority for faith and life, interpreting it together under Holy Spirit guidance, in the light of Jesus Christ, to discern God's will for our obedience.

5. The Spirit of Jesus empowers us to trust God in all areas of life so we become peacemakers who renounce violence, love our enemies, seek justice, and share our possessions with those in need.

6. We gather regularly to worship, to celebrate the Lord's Supper, and to hear the Word of God in a spirit of mutual accountability.

7. As a world-wide community of faith and life we transcend boundaries of nationality, race, class, gender and language. We seek to live in the world without conforming to the powers of evil, witnessing to God's grace by serving others, caring for creation, and inviting all people to know Jesus Christ as Saviour and Lord.

In these convictions we draw inspiration from Anabaptist forebears of the 16th century, who modelled radical discipleship to Jesus Christ. We seek to walk in his name by the power of the Holy Spirit, as we confidently await Christ's return and the final fulfillment of God's kingdom.

Adopted by Mennonite World Conference General Council, March 15, 2006

Notes

Chapter 1

1 Colin relays his experience from a trip to the Dominican Republic to consult a businessperson on how to best serve the people living in a garbage dump called La Canada in Santo Domingo.

2 World Hunger, "World Hunger Facts," accessed August 27, 2020, https:/www.worldhunger.org/world-child-hunger-facts/.

3 Martin Luther King Jr., "Letter from a Birmingham Jail," in *Why We Can't Wait* (New York: Penguin, 2000), 70. First published 1963.

4 See Genesis 3.

5 See Genesis 1:28-31, in which God gives Adam and Eve the blessed responsibility to rule ("subdue"/"dominion" in some versions of the Bible) over the earth. This by no means gives humans the right to abuse their power over the earth. In fact, the opposite is true. God's intention is for humanity to rule over God's creation for good. This means we have the responsibility to make sure we rule in God's favor according to his will for our earth. Any environmental, economic, racial, religious, political, or militaristic abuse against creation and humanity is an abuse of our God-given responsibility and is a grave injustice.

6 See Philippians 3:20-21.

Chapter 2

1 This famous quote is attributed to Lord Acton back in 1887.

2 "In Hobbema, Residential-School Survivors Share Their Stories with Commission," The *Globe and Mail*, accessed July 24, 2013, https://www.theglobeandmail.com/news/national/in-hobbema-residential-school-survivors-share-their-stories-with-commission/article13403496/.

3 See Office for Social Justice: Archdiocese of St. Paul and Minneapolis, "Catholic Social Teaching," Catholic Charities of St. Paul and Minneapolis, accessed August 27, 2020, https://www.cctwincities.org/education-advocacy/catholic-social-teaching/.

Chapter 3

1 Max Roser, "Global Economic Inequality," Our World in Data, November 24, 2013 https://ourworldindata.org/global-economic-inequality.

2 According to *Forbes* magazine, in 2016, "The top 1% of Americans pocketed 85% of total income growth, according to a study released from the Economic Policy Institute. As of 2013, the average family income of the top 1% was 25 times the average income for the other 99%." Lauren Debter, "What It Takes to Be Part of the One Percent,"*Forbes*, June 16, 2016, https://www.forbes.com/sites/laurengensler/2016/06/16/one-percent-by-state-income-inequality.

Chapter 4

1 Jesus' family was poor, as seen in the sacrifice they brought when Jesus was presented at the temple—see Luke 2:24 and compare it to Leviticus 12:8.

Chapter 5

1 Walter Brueggeman, "Voices of the Night—Against Injustice," in Walter Brueggeman, Sharon Parks, and Thomas H. Groome, *To Act Justly, Love Tenderly, Walk Humbly: A Minister's Agenda* (Eugene, OR: Wipf and Stock, 1997), 5.

2 The Hebrew word for "justice" is also translated "righteousness." Christians are called to make justice a priority in response to Jesus' invitation to "seek first his kingdom and his righteousness [justice]" (Matthew 6:33).

3 Gregory Boyle, *Tattoos on the Heart: The Power of Boundless Compassion* (New York: Simon and Schuster, 2010), 240.

4 Walter Wink, *The Powers That Be* (New York: Doubleday, 1999).

5 A favela is a slum.

Chapter 6

1 "Criminal Justice Fact Sheet," NAACP, accessed August 27, 2020, https://www.naacp.org/criminal-justice-fact-sheet/.

2 William Darity Jr., Darrick Hamilton, Mark Paul, Alan Aja, Anne Price, Antonio Moore, and Caterina Chiopris, "What We Get Wrong about Closing the Racial Wealth Gap," Samuel DuBois Cook Center on Racial Equity, Duke University, April 2018, https://socialequity.duke.edu/portfolio-item/what-we-get-wrong-about-closing-the-racial-wealth-gap/.

3 Risa Lavizzo-Mourey and David Williams, "Being Black Is Bad for Your Health," *US News and World Report*, April 14, 2016, https://www.usnews.com/opinion/blogs/policy-dose/articles/2016-04-14/theres-a-huge-health-equity-gap-between-whites-and-minorities.

4 Sarah Mervosh, "How Much Wealthier Are White School Districts Than Nonwhite Ones? $23 Billion, Report Says," *New York Times*, February 27, 2019, https://www.nytimes.com/2019/02/27/education/school-districts-funding-white-minorities.html.

5 "Health Disparities between Blacks and Whites Run Deep," Harvard T. H. Chang School of Public Health, April 15, 2016, https://www.hsph.harvard.edu/news/hsph-in-the-news/health-disparities-between-blacks-and-whites-run-deep/.

6 Michelle Alexander, *The New Jim Crow: Mass Incarceration in the Age of Colorblindness* (New York: The New Press, 2012), 63–69.

7 Ibid., 98–99.

8 Ibid., 89.

9 Ibid., 98.

10 Ibid., 106.

11 Brenda Salter McNeil, *Becoming Brave: Finding the Courage to Pursue Racial Justice Now* (Grand Rapids, MI: Brazos Press, 2020).

12 Ibid.

13 Vincent Harding, "The Beggars Are Marching . . . Where Are the Saints?," in Joanna Shenk, *The Movement Makes Us Human: An Interview with Dr. Vincent Harding on Mennonites, Vietnam, and MLK* (Eugene, OR: Wipf and Stock, 2018), 94–95.

14 Fannie Lou Hamer, "We're On Our Way" (speech, Indianola, MS, September 1964), Voices of Democracy, https://voicesofdemocracy .umd.edu/hamer-were-on-our-way-speech-text/.

15 Ruby Sales, "Where Does It Hurt?," interview by Krista Tippett, *On Being with Krista Tippett*, WNYC Studios, last modified January 16, 2020, https://onbeing.org/programs/ruby-sales-where-does-it-hurt/.

16 Martin Luther King Jr., "Loving Your Enemies" (sermon, Dexter Baptist Church, Montgomery, AL, November 17, 1957).

17 Ibid.

The Authors

Colin McCartney has worked in urban missions for over thirty-five years. He is the founder of two urban ministries and the author of two books, *The Beautiful Disappointment* and *Red Letter Revolution*. He has appeared on Canadian television and radio and published articles in national newspapers regarding urban issues. He is a mentor to pastors and businesspeople and serves as a ministry trainer and coach. He is also a popular speaker and currently leads an urban church planting movement called Connect City.

Judith McCartney's greatest passion is to support and develop people to create change together.

Judith is a graduate of Arrow Leadership and has a master's degree in leadership and management from Briercrest Seminary. She is also an urban ministry veteran and church planter and is currently the pastor of SoulHouse Church in Toronto, Ontario. Judith is deeply involved in mentoring young leaders in the areas of social justice and self-care, with a heart for young women in leadership.

Both Colin and Judith serve together as partners in ministry in Toronto, and have two grown children. Connect with them at www.connectcity.org.

SMALL BOOKS

THE
JESUS
WAY

of RADICAL FAITH

**What Is the Bible and
How Do We Understand It?**

by Dennis R. Edwards

**Why Did Jesus Die and What
Difference Does It Make?**

by Michele Hershberger

**What Is the Trinity
and Why Does It Matter?**

by Steve Dancause

**Why Do We Suffer and
Where Is God When We Do?**

by Valerie G. Rempel

**Who Are Our Enemies and
How Do We Love Them?**

by Hyung Jin Kim Sun

**What Does Justice
Look Like and Why
Does God Care about It?**

by Judith and Colin McCartney

**What Is God's Mission in the
World and How Do We Join It?**

by Juan F. Martínez and Jamie Pitts

(SPRING 2021)

**What Is the Church
and Why Does It Exist?**

by David Fitch

(SPRING 2021)

**What Is God's Kingdom
and What Does
Citizenship Look Like?**

by César García

(SPRING 2021)

**Who Was Jesus and What
Does It Mean to Follow Him?**

by Nancy Elizabeth Bedford

(SPRING 2021)

HERALD
PRESS

www.HeraldPress.com. 1-800-245-7894